THE LEADERSHIP LIBRARY
V O L U M E   8
PREACHING TO CONVINCE

THE LEADERSHIP LIBRARY

Volume
8

Preaching to Convince

James D. Berkley, ed.

Carol Stream, Illinois

WORD BOOKS
PUBLISHER
WACO, TEXAS

A DIVISION OF
WORD, INCORPORATED

PREACHING TO CONVINCE

Introduction, chapter introductions, and ancillary copy ©1986 Christianity Today, Inc.

Chapter 1 ©1985 Tim Timmons
Chapter 2 ©1983 Fred Smith
Chapter 3 ©1983 Haddon Robinson
Chapter 4 ©1984 Calvin Miller
Chapter 5 ©1984 Christianity Today, Inc.
Chapter 6 ©1984 William Kruidenier
Chapter 7 ©1983 Mark Littleton
Chapter 8 ©1983 Jamie Buckingham
Chapter 9 ©1983 Gordon MacDonald
Chapter 10 ©1986 David Mains
Chapter 11 ©1984 Leighton Ford
Chapter 12 ©1982 Ben Patterson
Chapter 13 ©1981 Warren Wiersbe

A LEADERSHIP/Word Book. Copublished by Christianity Today, Inc. and Word, Inc. Distributed by Word Books

Cover art by Joe Van Severen

Library of Congress Cataloging-in-Publication Data

Preaching to convince.

(The Leadership library ; v. 8)
"A Leadership/Word book"——T.p. verso.
1. Preaching. I. Berkley, James D., 1950-
II. Series.
BV4211.2.P738 1986   251   86-17173
ISBN 0-917463-11-0

Printed in the United States of America

To my wife,
Deborah:
my favorite sermon coach,
whom I'm grateful I convinced
to accept the role.

CONTENTS

INTRODUCTION

Preaching: that exquisite agony. How we love it in the pulpit when, to borrow Olympic runner Eric Liddell's phrase, "we feel God's pleasure." How exquisite when the Word takes root and people's lives are changed. Yet, what agony on Tuesday morning when we try feebly to wrest some cogent meaning out of a Levitical text. How preaching terrorizes us late Saturday night when the sermon still won't gel.

During my ten years as a pastor, I learned that preaching is a love-hate affair for most of those who speak Sunday after Sunday. It is hard and holy work.

What other of our endeavors is so often a victim of cheap humor? What other task has been so called into question in this "hot" communication era? Where else do we experience such ambivalence?

Yet, where but in the church do people's lives so change simply by listening? Who but the preacher assembles such a regular and willing audience — people expecting a challenge?

Certainly the sermon is here to stay. It works. Lives are forever lifted. The Word flourishes with transforming power. And that is the assumption of this book. We can preach to convince.

That implies that convincing is *legitimate*. With the bad name "propagandizing" bears, some have called into question the very notion of convincing others. "Let people do their own thing," we hear. "Let's not impose our morality on them." Mind-bending cults and consciousness-altering drugs have bred distrust about anything that "interferes" with another's freedom of thought. Much of society outside the church maintains a relativistic, hands-off approach to the convictions of others.

The apostle Paul never felt that way. He spent his last months in Rome trying to change minds: "From morning till evening he explained and declared to them the kingdom of God and tried to convince them about Jesus" (Acts 28:23). In Corinth, Paul "reasoned in the synagogue, trying to persuade Jews and Greeks" (Acts 18:4). He wanted the Corinthian church to have proper order in worship so that an outsider would "be convinced by all that he is a sinner" and fall down and worship God (1 Cor. 14:24–25). Preaching to convince was the order of the day in the early church.

Preaching moves beyond merely imparting information to impassioned convincing that demands a personal response. That, perhaps, is one difference between teaching and preaching. Preaching without convincing is like cooking a meal that no one eats. We need make no apologies for preaching to convince.

If such preaching is necessary, it is also *difficult*. Even Niccolo Machiavelli, the master of manipulation, found "there is nothing more difficult to take in hand, more perilous to conduct, or more uncertain in its success, than to take the lead in the introduction of a new order of things." Convincing people to change remains neither our simplest nor safest undertaking.

Persuasion theorists in social psychology have accumulated a number of tricks of the trade for would-be convincers: identify with the audience, utilize presumed authority, coattail on the goodwill of a third party. Yet, while appropriating all we can from such research, we would still be at a loss if it weren't for the transforming power of the Holy Spirit to use even our worst efforts to realign lives. Preaching to convince is difficult, but not overwhelming when we tap the right Source.

Best of all, preaching to convince *works*. From the thousands at Pentecost who were "cut to the heart" and asked Peter, "What shall we do?" to the young John Wesley whose "heart was strangely warmed" by the inelegant reading of the preface to a commentary on Romans, to saints in Syracuse and Sioux City and Salinas who hear God's Word preached and turn to him, sermons continue to convince hearers and move them to transformed lives and rearranged priorities.

Several years ago the *British Weekly* printed a letter to the editor:

Dear Sir:
    I notice that ministers seem to set a great deal of importance on their sermons and spend a great deal of time in preparing them. I have been attending services quite regularly for the past thirty years and during that time, if I estimate correctly, I have listened to no less than three thousand sermons. But, to my consternation, I discover I cannot remember a single one of them. I wonder if a minister's time might be more profitably spent on something else?
    Sincerely . . .

That letter triggered an avalanche of angry responses for weeks. Sermons were castigated and defended by lay and clergy, but eventually a single letter closed the debate:

My Dear Sir:
    I have been married for thirty years. During that time I have eaten 32,850 meals — mostly of my wife's cooking. Suddenly I have discovered that I cannot remember the menu of a single meal. And yet, I received nourishment from every one of them. I have the distinct impression that without them, I would have starved to death long ago.
    Sincerely . . .

Many will wander off unfed and will starve without those who preach to convince. In this menu planner, we have attempted to provide the best assistance to those anxious to feed their flocks. The chapters come from the hearts and ministries of individuals who preach regularly and know the exquisite agony of the pulpit. They are convinced that preaching matters, that they have something well worth the effort to convince their people to believe. The sections on preparing, proclaiming, illustrating, concluding, and reflecting give us nourishment for our preaching, to the end that all may be convinced that Jesus Christ is Lord.

— James D. Berkley
Associate Editor
LEADERSHIP

O N E

WHY SHOULD THEY LISTEN TO ME?

To stand and drone out a sermon in a kind of articulate snoring to people who are somewhat between awake and asleep must be wretched work.

CHARLES HADDON SPURGEON

The apostle Paul wrote, "How can people hear without someone preaching to them?" Tim Timmons wonders, "How do we make them even want to hear?"

No preacher wants to preach to empty pews or vacant stares.

In our day, we cannot assume the sermon will fall upon willing ears. In some circles, sermon is a dirty word. "Don't preach to me!" is practically the motto of a generation. Gone are the days when the great sermons were broadly read and discussed. Today, preachers must capture the ears of the crowd if they will be heard at all among the cacophony of compact discs and Coke commercials.

Timmons, immersed in the life of Irvine, California — the capital of Southern California chic — has spied out the unpromising land of secular life. At South Coast Community Church, swirling, shifting, unsettled secularity surrounds him. He knows the shuttle buses run to Disneyland and Newport Beach rather than his church. So why would anyone come to hear his preaching?

Timmons has found a method. And people do flock to hear him preach — people who could be polishing their convertibles or jogging under graceful palms or enhancing their year-round tans.

This first chapter tackles a question prior to any convincing the preacher might accomplish: "Why should they listen to me?"

A fellow attended a special evening service at the church but sat near the door. After the speaker had droned on for some forty minutes, the fellow got up and left. On the way out, he met a friend coming in. The man asked, "Am I very late, Zeke? What's he talking about?"

"Don't know. He ain't said yet!"

In every speaking situation, what matters most is this: Did the audience get the speaker's point?

I know no greater misery than sensing the audience isn't listening to me. It makes me so nervous I talk faster, pound the pulpit or raise my voice, and seem flooded with perspiration from every pore! In 1971 a friend, Rabbi White, invited me to speak to the national officers of the Jewish Defense League. Now the J.D.L. is no tea-and-crumpets group. They tend to get physical. What's worse, Rabbi White asked me to speak on "Why I Believe Jesus Is the Messiah!" I can think of at least three million better ideas.

To be honest, nothing worked that day. As I spoke, they seemed to size up my body thinking, *One grenade should do it.* They had no intention of listening.

After many experiences of saying too much to people who

listen too little, I have made it my life's goal to *talk so people will listen*. From my experience with secular audiences and Christian congregations, I carved out an approach I call the "AHAAAA! Method of Communication." (That's because my aim is to move the audience to an "AHAAAA!" response.) The method has six steps:

Define Your Audience

No speaker is more effective than the one who knows and relates to an audience, yet few things are more difficult. As we emerge from our theological training stuffed with "all the answers," it's very easy to preach answers to people not asking those questions. And until I know the questions, the answers don't matter.

When requested to speak, I ask five basic questions:

First, who is my audience (age, sex, background, prejudices)?

Second, what are their questions (thoughts, feelings, struggles, pains, needs)?

Third, which of those questions shall I address?

Fourth, what is God's answer to this question?

And fifth, how much time do I have?

These help me relate to my listeners, whether for a series of messages or a one-shot opportunity.

When I first moved to California, I delivered one of my most memorable messages to a community group. I was so impressed with my intellectual prowess. I traced the line of despair à la Schaeffer. I made monkeys out of evolutionists à la Wilder-Smith. I proved humanism inhuman à la Montgomery. I dazzled them with my footwork — dazzled them to sleep. Why? Simply because I was so into my "answers" I forgot to get into their questions.

How does one discover the questions? The most effective way I know is to live with people. I enjoy this most about the pastorate. I live among those I pastor and those I want to reach. For years I stepped all around people to go speak here and there. But for the last ten years I have been *living with people* in my world. There's a big difference.

This means *thinking with them*, reading what they are reading — best sellers, self-help books, insight books, psychological books, magazines, newsletters, and anything else I can get my hands on that will help me understand people. I want to know their struggles and pains — their questions. Once I understand their questions, I can package relevant biblical answers for distribution.

Another helpful activity is to *speak frequently in secular situations*. If my aim is to reach my community, I can say yes to Rotary, Kiwanis, Exchange Club, Junior League, P.T.A., and many other civic organizations that constantly seek speakers. Taking advantage of these opportunities forces me to think about this kind of audience. It's a great exercise in analysis.

I must also *play with them*. Just as Jesus went to the "sinners," so we must go where people need the Lord — the health club, tennis club, YMCA, racquetball court, or country club. Community soccer, baseball, basketball, and football programs are always in need of volunteers. Coaching soccer and baseball each year gives me close contact with several entire families for a season.

Fourth, I must *counsel with them*. By this I am not insisting on a line-up of appointments. However, if I talk so people listen, I will stir up more and more questions, and they will seek further help. Here I grapple with people's pain — their lostness. Nothing escorts me into reality more quickly than being eyeball-to-eyeball with a family's seemingly impossible situation. When I'm standing in the midst of a hemorrhage, my spiritual Band-Aids seem to shrink a bit.

I think of my task this way: If I don't relate to my world, my world will never relate to my God.

Determine the Handicaps

I've found three ongoing handicaps that tend to keep us from talking so people will listen. If we are not aware of these handicaps, we will not work on them. And if we don't, they will virtually silence our message.

The first is that *the world is listening to everything else*. There is no such thing as a captive audience. Competition nearly overwhelms people; they suffer from overcommitment and overchoice. In my community, people have almost stopped signing up for things in advance; they just show up — *if* there is nothing better to do.

Our world also suffers from the greatest religion of all — confusionism. People are confused about right and wrong, relationships, the future as well as the past. They are also confused about identity, the mystery of intimacy, and their struggle with inadequacy. And for the most part, the Bible isn't recognized as a primary authority. It's just another voice in the confusion.

To overcome this handicap, we must offer clear, pertinent answers to the world's greatest needs. The Bible must be demonstrated as a relevant, down-to-earth message of healing.

The second handicap is that *the church is talking to itself*. We create evangelistic programs and air them on Christian stations. We write evangelistic articles and print them in Christian magazines. We publish evangelistic books and sell them only in Christian bookstores. We have evangelistic meetings and hold them within the four holy walls of the church facility. Then we are shocked when the world doesn't listen.

We must take this handicap seriously. If we are to be salt and light interrelating with people in our world to bring them to a personal relationship with Jesus Christ, we must prepare and present our life-changing message for those who need it most. We have been judging the world and talking to ourselves when we really ought to be judging ourselves and talking to the world — in ways they will listen.

The third handicap is that *the speaker is in a box*. It seems every Christian group has its "holy huddle." Their whole purpose is to hold on until Jesus returns. They are not interested in talking so people will listen, because they believe no one ever will listen. Such people will embalm our ministry if we let them. We must love them, care for them, and listen to them, but never allow ourselves to be managed by them.

Another box is formed by our influential professors and past mentors. The first few years out of seminary I found myself still speaking, writing, and counseling for my professors. It was as if they were still with me, looking over my shoulder and evaluating me. This blurred my primary audience.

Defeating this handicap means being managed only by God, not the "holy huddle" or past professors. Then we are freed to respond to the real audience.

Direct the Angle

With my audience and handicaps in mind, I next choose my subject matter and aim it appropriately. Jesus always directed what he wanted to say toward his audience. To the woman at the well, the angle was the water of life. To the blind man, it was the light of the world.

In a world riddled with problems, we must not teach the Word of God without angling our teaching toward those desperate problems. Alcoholism, drug abuse, divorce, child molestation, crime, suicide, and disease are all epidemic, and Christians are not sealed in a mayonnaise jar against them. To get the "AHAAAA!" response from our congregations, we must direct the angle of our message toward their problems.

Develop Your Attitude

The more I speak the more I realize that people tune in to my attitude before they listen to anything I have to say. They catch my attitudes about two things: myself and humanity.

If I affect a pious sanctity, they are unable to identify and will not listen. But when my attitude is genuinely down-to-earth, the barriers come down. My vulnerability is vital to getting people to listen. They must be able to trust me.

People won't miss my attitude toward humanity in general, either. I want my audience to know I care for them no matter what. That's hard to resist. I want to express this attitude: *I'm not OK, you're not OK, and that's OK, because there is hope to become OK through a personal relationship with God.*

At a tennis club one day nearly two years ago, my scheduled opponent didn't show up. Another match was arranged for me. We introduced ourselves and moved to our respective back lines to warm up.

Suddenly the man said, "What was your name again?"

"Tim Timmons."

He dropped his racquet and moved toward the net. I met him there. With a finger pointing into my face, he asked repeatedly, "Do you know who I am?"

"No," I said, "I don't."

"Are you sure?"

"Yes, I'm sure!"

Finally he blurted out, "I'm going to tell you: I'm the porno king of Orange County! What do you think of that?"

I could tell he was waiting for me to pull a big, black Bible out of my sports bag and tear into him.

I put my finger up into his face and said, "Let me ask *you* something. Can you play tennis?"

He gulped and eventually mumbled, "Yes."

"Then get back there, and *let's play!*" I said. We went at it. I prayed in that instance for victory (a Grade A miracle) and surprisingly, my prayers were answered.

When he shook my hand at the net, his first words were "What times are your services Sunday?" He began attending, and in six months, he retired from the pornography business. About eight months later he placed his faith in Jesus. What a thrill to watch all this! Because he bought my attitude toward him and life in general, he was willing to listen to my message.

Deliver Your Appeals

At this point, the audience is ready to listen. Now what will they hear?

We must appeal to them, and our appeal must be dynamic.

While the audience is a crucial determinant of *what* to present, our intended appeal is the pivotal factor in *how* to deliver a message. The appeals we make are the basic connectors between us and our audience. If executed properly, they enable us to break down the invisible wall between us.

The nature of these appeals makes the difference between true *persuasion* and shameless *propaganda*. Persuasion moves people to change on a long-term basis in view of great reward. The shift is genuine. Propaganda moves people to change on a short-term basis, usually producing great regret. It's the skilled art of the con man hyping his audience for an instant, with no one to fix the wreckage.

Every time I stand up to speak, my listeners ask one foundational question: *Why should I listen to you?* And within this question are three subquestions:

Can I trust you?
Do you care for me?
Do you know what you are talking about?

Unless I answer all three adequately, I greatly hinder any opportunity for true persuasion. On the contrary, if I answer each of these well, I have the best opportunity to communicate dynamically and truly persuade.

The question *Can I trust you?* amounts to *Are you a good person? Have you experienced what you're talking about? What are you really selling?* My audience wants to know my *ethical appeal.*

Ethical appeal is not easily put on. You either have it or you don't. It is normally based on a good track record. People can smell it. Those who have it smell good; those who don't smell bad. And audiences are sniffing away, because they must pick up the scent of ethical appeal before they will respond.

In the recent Billy Graham Crusade in Anaheim, California, I was challenged again by his incredible ethical appeal. He really doesn't have to say much (though he does), nor does he have to say it in a dynamic way (though he does). He overwhelms his audience with his long track record of ethical appeal.

The second subquestion, *Do you care for me?* is a short way of saying, *Are you interested primarily in your own well-being or mine? Do you mean what you say? Are you actually committed to it? Are you excited about it?* My audience wants to know my *emotional appeal.* Do I really care for them, or am I just going through the motions? People sense enthusiasm and intensity. Emotional appeal becomes contagious, and the audience has a tough time resisting it.

Over the years I watched Richard Halverson demonstrate vibrant emotional appeal to his congregation in Bethesda, Maryland. Each Sunday he expressed his true excitement and affection for his people. He told them how much he loved them and appreciated the privilege of being their pastor. He had one of the most beautiful love affairs with his congregation I've ever seen.

Third, *Do you know what you are talking about? Do you make sense? Do you have evidence? Is that evidence fair? Who are your authorities?* My audience wants to know my *logical appeal.* This does not mean telling all I know about a subject, but it must be clear that I know much more than I am telling. Logical appeal helps an audience understand truth more clearly and persuades them that it makes enough sense to act upon it.

I have found it extremely effective to appeal to secular authorities as part of my logical appeal. There are biblical examples of this technique, especially Paul's use of Greek poets in his Acts 17 address in Athens. Using the Word of God as a foundational authority, it's easy to find widely accepted secular references that state the same truth. This does not make the biblical truth more true, but it does lead your audience from the secular authority they already accept to your ultimate authority they may or may not already accept.

Probably the clearest example of all three appeals in action is in 1 Thessalonians 2:1–13. Paul approached his audience "not . . . from error or impurity or by way of deceit . . . nor with a pretext for greed." (Ethical appeal — *Can I trust you?*) He also approached them "as a nursing mother tenderly cares for her own children. . . ." (Emotional appeal — *Do you care for me?*) Having laid this foundation, his logical appeal was successful; he says, "When you received from us the word of God's message, you accepted it not as the word of men, but for what it really is, the word of God."

That's what I want as a response to my communication. This is what I mean by "AHAAAA!" — an ethically, emotionally, and logically satisfying response to God's truth.

Do Application

Application becomes natural if it follows the preceding steps. As a speaker, I simply must not ignore the action-steps that flow out of a message. I have heard it said that 5 percent of an audience are innovators, 15 percent are adapters, and 80 percent are adopters. If this is even approximately accurate, most of our audiences will not act on their own. They need simple action-steps they can adopt to apply truth.

I test my action-steps with a three-point quiz:

First, are they *realistic?* Can people actually do them? Would *I* do them?

Second, are the steps *relational?* Is anybody else committed to them? Without a dimension of relational accountability, most applications of truth seem to have a built-in fizzle factor.

Third, are my action-steps *responsible?* Do they lead people toward greater personal responsibility? I don't want to leave any room for my audience to blame others or count on them unduly for help.

After all is said and done, more is said than done. Our task as pastors is to close that gap between talking and walking. The most effective gap-closing method I know is to talk so more people will listen, moving them toward a satisfied "AHAAAA!" response.

T W O

DOES ANYONE KNOW WHAT CREATIVE MEANS?

Most people think once or twice in a lifetime. I've made a reputation of thinking once or twice a month.

H. G. WELLS

"Every time I turn around, it's Sunday!"
You know the feeling. Wasn't it just yesterday you last preached? And now another sermon stares you in the face. Time again to be wise, profound, and creative. Especially creative.

How do you do it? Telling people to be creative is about like asking them to stand on a stage and act natural. We don't simply turn on creativity. We can't buy it or borrow it.

Yet we still desire creativity, for without it the sermon barrel empties and the minds in the pews switch to PAUSE. *Without a fresh and interesting approach to each sermon, we preach not to convince; we preach to concrete.*

Fred Smith has learned that creativity can be cultivated. Smith is a career businessman in Dallas, Texas, with a lifelong love affair with the church. His own creativity rests not in paintbrush or guitar but in his ability to see things with clarity and cast new light on hackneyed practices.

In this chapter, he ventures some thoughts about developing that much-desired attribute — creativity.

Т he word *creative* has become a cliché. Everybody uses it whether he can define it or not. Creativity is expected of ministers no less than of advertising copywriters and fashion designers. If you're not certified "creative," your future is in big trouble.

The blunt fact, of course, is that no one is creative. We live in a closed universe; there is nothing new under the sun. What we are instead is *inventive*; we rearrange and reposition things that have already been created.

Throughout this chapter I will use the words *creative* and *creativity* even though what I am talking about is inventiveness. This will seem more natural to our speech patterns. And I hope the Creator will not be offended.

Creativity has to do with more than just the arts — painting, sculpture, music, architecture. In my view, *creativity is survival*. When an institution loses its transitional quality in a moving market, a moving culture, a moving world, it doesn't survive. The railroad industry wanted to stay as railroad companies rather than transportation companies. The transition was toward airplanes and private automobiles, but they liked railroading. Many went out of business.

In the parachurch we have some excellent examples of using creative solutions to satisfy spiritual needs: Torrey Johnson saw wandering crowds of World War II soldiers looking for something to do on the streets of Chicago, so he created Youth for Christ. When secularism swept the West Coast campuses in the sixties, Campus Crusade for Christ was the creative answer. Bill Glass, All-Pro football player, found prisoners wouldn't come to hear preaching, so he started sports clinics for them.

I've been depressed recently by a statistic from a major denomination: the average tenure of its pastors is now eighteen months. When I asked why, the answer was "Because that's about how many sermons they have." By the end of eighteen months, they've preached to the bottom of the barrel, and the only choice is to move.

Apparently no springs of creativity have been nurtured so that new (or at least repositioned) things are bubbling up from inside. That's why I say that for people in leadership, creativity is not a luxury; it's survival.

Eight Essential Qualities

Those who may rightly be called creative show the following characteristics:

1. *Wide association.* While most new ideas are conceived by a single person sitting alone, such a moment does not tell the whole story. The truly creative people I know stay in touch with other creative people. Bright ideas may hit them at three in the morning, but they come out of an environment of creativity.

You have to set up an almost constant discipline to maintain your vitality through association. Creative people ask you the right kind of questions. They probe you. So you stay in touch with them.

2. *Special areas.* Ralph Carmichael, the trend-setting Christian musician, and I were talking about marketing one day, and he said, "Fred, if you want to talk fast to me, talk music. I

can talk music fast, but I have to talk business slow." I know exactly what he meant, because it's the opposite with me! In the area of a person's gift, he can race along. His pores are open. He knows all the nuances and ramifications; problems in this area excite him.

When I find individuals trying to function in an area that threatens them, I usually say, "This must not be your area." People who battle stage fright shouldn't be public speakers. All good speakers have nervousness, yes, but they are able to use it. It creates energy; it revs up the mind. Christian leaders who are immobilized by the big problems of their lives should question whether they're working in their area of strength.

John R. W. Stott says expository preaching is chewing on a verse like a dog on a bone. I'd advise most ministers not to spend their time in that way because they're not John Stott or G. Campbell Morgan. If you're not creative in finding new meanings in the nooks and corners of Scripture, then put your energy into another area. I'd hate to see a tremendous communicator like Chuck Swindoll spend time gnawing on individual verses. He's far more creative at mixing words and pictures to convey old truth in a new and vital way.

3. *Dissatisfaction.* Some people call it noble discontent. Whatever its name, creative people are infested with the idea that the way things are being done today is not the way they can be done best.

Roger Bannister didn't believe a mile run had to take four minutes. Something inside told him that if he'd break down the mile into four separate parts and go to work on each quarter of the mile, he could cut off seconds. Now, of course, four minutes is old and slow.

That spirit of discontent is crucial to creativity. I'm trying to instill it in my grandson, who plays golf with me occasionally. He loves the game, and when he gets off a good drive down the fairway, he'll say, "Perfect."

"No, Greg," I'll say. "It's good, but it's not perfect."

"Well, it went where I wanted it to go."

"Yes, but it didn't go where it could have gone."

We don't have to be negative or critical to be dissatisfied. Van Gogh was both creative and miserable — that's not what I mean. We can believe in a positive way that everything can be better. Every organization can be improved, every formula perfected.

Once I asked chemist George Schweitzer, "Why do scientists revere Einstein?"

"Because he put more formula into one formula than any other scientist."

"Well, what's the aim of all science?" I asked.

"To put everything into one formula."

What a challenge! No wonder great scientists are dissatisfied.

Great preachers and theologians are dissatisfied, too, not because they want to be authors of truth, but because they want to expand it, to understand it more fully, to rearrange it so people can utilize it better.

One minister asked me, "How do I develop creativity?"

I replied, "Pick out a few of your common problems and think of all the various ways to solve them. You'll have to think very hard, but do it anyway." When Robert McNamara was president of Ford, he would assign his associates problems to work out, and when they would come in to report, McNamara would say, "Now I'm sure this isn't the first solution you thought of. What was another one?" It was his way of forcing everyone to think of at least two ways to solve every problem.

Creative people love to have options. They love to drive home a different route each day. They refuse to drop down on the floor like a toddler and start crying, "I can't." They know there are multiple ways to do almost everything.

If you don't give yourself a lot of options to consider, how do you know which one's best? One of the reasons I'm convinced of original sin is that I rarely see anyone accomplish the best the first time. If there weren't some basic problem with humanity, writers wouldn't have to rewrite their material five times, engineers wouldn't have to return to the drawing board, and preachers wouldn't have to rebuild sermon out-

lines from scratch. It takes awhile, but eventually quality floats to the top if we are dissatisfied long enough.

4. *Awe.* An expanding concept of God and his world is another part of creativity. While dissatisfaction moves us toward *change*, awe moves us toward *exploration*. The great astronomers can hardly change what they see in space, but they are moved by awe to explore it, nevertheless.

I'll never forget traveling as a young man from my native Tennessee up to New York City. Standing on the corner of Fifty-seventh Street and Sixth Avenue one day, I suddenly realized the situation was beyond me. There was simply no way to know all those people, as I did back home. I was overwhelmed. The God I had brought along was too small. He had to be bigger than I thought to take in a place like New York.

From that time, I have had an expanding concept of God. This has not intimidated me; rather, it has pulled me along to grow creatively as I see more and more of him.

5. *High physical and mental energy.* A lot of people have wonderful ideas but lack the energy to explore them. Einstein once said nature holds almost no secrets that cannot be found out by prolonged concentration and intense study. We only have to bear down.

Some creative people bear down so hard that they burn out early in life. Some of the great musicians died very young, for example, as did some inventors. Others have lived longer but found they couldn't burn the midnight oil like they used to. All of them were — to be honest — unbalanced. They couldn't help it when they became fascinated with an idea.

One of the most fortunate things in life is when a highly creative spirit comes in a highly energetic body. Let others criticize if they will; great things will result.

And when they do, the creative person will supply his or her own strokes. Some of the most creative solutions I have found in my business were things only I knew about. The acclaim of others was not necessary; I knew I had solved a problem.

6. *The ability to think in principles.* Less than 10 percent of the population can do this, I'm told; most think only in techniques. And I don't really know how to develop this ability. I only know I can recognize it by listening to a person.

If a speaker thinks in principles, he shows it by his breadth of illustration. He draws from many different fields, not just his particular specialty, because he sees the principles that weave throughout. If a speaker always tells stories from one field, or if his illustrations do not extrapolate accurately, then we know he does not understand the principle.

Mathematicians talk about the elegant answer and the grotesque answer. I mentioned to one mathematician that I had never liked math in school. "I can understand that," he said, "because they taught you the grotesqueness of arithmetic instead of the elegance of mathematics." Great mathematicians work through the welter of technique until they come to a marvelous principle; pi, for example, or the discovery of the zero, which happened in India and revolutionized our ability to work with numbers.

This, incidentally, is why many great mathematicians are musicians. They have moved past drudgery and grotesqueness to elegance.

At a university conference on business, I was scheduled to speak after the dean of engineering. He opened his speech by saying, "I am a scientist. I deal only with hard facts — things you can see and feel."

When it was my turn, I said, "I don't mean to be discourteous, but most of life is made up of soft facts. I respect hard facts, but when I take the long view, I notice that the rocks and the riverbank do not control the water that flows in the stream; the water forms the rocks and the bank.

"All matters of the spirit are soft, but they ultimately control. Armies, formulas, and scientific technology do not guarantee that a civilization will survive. That is up to other factors. The soft is just as factual as the hard, but more difficult to deal with."

In the ministry, we are constantly dealing with the power of soft facts. When we see that as a principle, then we can start to think creatively about it.

7. *A style that is uninhibited (but not undisciplined).* Creative people cannot let themselves be hemmed in by tradition.

A member of the Tarrytown Group said recently, "The world is between trapezes. We're leaving the one we have known and trying to catch one we do not know." I like that metaphor. We often feel that way about our own lives. Maybe life is a series of trapeze jumps; maybe each day is a new trapeze. Certainly the creative person is always leaving one trapeze and hurtling toward the next.

We Christians limit ourselves too much. To me, the Bible has always been a compass. I am not afraid to wander in anybody's woods so long as I have a compass.

I have friends who are unbelievers, and some of them never do get out of the woods. Others get out only by chance. But with a compass, you can relax; you can wander far off the paths, because any time you need to get out, you can. You can feel competent to wander in almost any company, any group, any set of ideas, because you have Scripture to guide you out at the necessary moment.

Too many Christians are worried about the wagon instead of the load. If any idea comes in a wagon they don't like, they reject the load without even looking it over. I don't care whether creativity comes from an atheist, an agnostic, a liberal, or whomever — if the idea is good, I want it, and I'm not going to fuss about the mode of transportation.

Being uninhibited, however, does not mean being out of control. A vice-president of General Motors once told me, "We want people with disciplined imaginations." A leader, though tremendously creative, cannot be loose in his behavior.

Pastors are sometimes caught in a unique squeeze when their attempts to be free in ministry are read by the congregation in behavioral terms only. Take Sunday morning, for example. Many Christians have gotten to the place that the eleven o'clock service is nothing more than a ritual. There's no spiritual vitality; there is only habit. This problem has to be solved very, very slowly.

A dear friend of mine, pastor of a large church, a man of great integrity, came to the pulpit one Sunday morning and said, "You look to me for God's message. I have struggled all week, and God has given me no message. Therefore, let us stand and be dismissed."

If I had been there, I would have stood and applauded.

But he almost got thrown out of his church. Although he had done the honest thing, people were outraged. Some had brought friends that day — not to hear a message from God, but to hear their preacher. And he didn't perform.

He did invite them all back to the evening service, for which he felt he had a message. He delivered it that night as expected.

While such a shock may be dangerous, it is imperative that we work gradually but steadily toward making Sunday morning more than ritual. As a guest speaker, I can tell a dramatic difference in audiences. Some have been trained to listen — really listen — and others have not.

The other day I was invited to do a laymen's service in a church that usually has mediocre preaching. (The reason I know is that the pastor told me he dreads no day like Sunday.) As I spoke that day, I was half through before they started listening. What a contrast with a church like Key Biscayne Presbyterian in Florida, where they hang on every cough. The people are so used to listening intently that a guest is fascinated by the immediate attention his words receive. This kind of discipline takes time.

But it can be built. Most big problems are not solved fast.

A young pastor here in Dallas has decided to open the floor for ten minutes of questions following his sermon each week. It's most stimulating; he gets some hard queries now, because people have come to believe he wants them. He isn't opening up the service to be complimented, but to clarify. The problem he is attacking is people going home misunderstanding what the preacher said.

That's creative.

Sunday morning problems must be attacked creatively and diplomatically, but always with an eye toward the ultimate goal of vitality. Our thinking must be uninhibited, even when our behavior is not.

8. *Evaluation.* I know brainstorming is supposed to be a marvelous technique for creativity, but I think it is a silly fad. To sit around spouting ideas with no evaluation makes fools of everyone. Disciplined creativity must ask the following questions:

• "Is this practical?" Does this solution make enough difference to be worth the time and energy it will cost?

Will Rogers once listened to an admiral describe the menace of German U-boats during the First World War. Eventually, Rogers raised his hand and asked, "Tell me, can those things operate in boiling water?"

"No," the admiral replied, "I'm sure they can't."

"Well, then," said Rogers, "you've got your solution. Just boil the ocean."

The admiral gave him a blank stare and then muttered, "How?"

Rogers smiled, "I gave you the idea — you work out the details."

• The second question is "Does this violate scriptural principles?" I make a subtle difference between fulfilling the Bible's principles and not violating them. I probably will never understand the Scripture fully enough to meet all that it teaches, but in my motives I can at least keep from being dishonest.

• "Is this factual?" Does it coincide with truth, the way the world really is? Christians can live in fantasy land as easily as non-Christians. The love of truth is more of a scholarly trait than a religious trait, and we must all cultivate an absolute dedication to facts.

These are just three of the checkpoints creative people must employ. Most of us are fortunate to have one good idea out of ten, and so we must screen out the nine. We must be willing to submit them to the judgment of other people, who will help us.

I was bouncing a new thought off a lawyer friend one day, and I'll always remember the way he smiled and said, "Fred . . . that's not one of your better ideas." He did me a great service. I've used his line ever since with others who have brought their creative ideas to me for assessment.

Pastors and boards must do this work together. When a pastor or a deacon says, "I know I'm right. Sometimes you have to stand with God though everyone else stands against you," he is flirting with arrogance. Theoretically he may be correct, but in most cases he needs to listen to the evaluation of colleagues.

Does God Inhibit Creativity?

If you were to conduct a street interview on whether Christians or non-Christians are more creative, I have a hunch the majority would vote for the non-Christians. That is partly because they think uninhibited *behavior* is a sign of creativity, when actually it is a sign of rebellion.

Christians are constrained in their behavior, but that does not need to transfer to their thinking. If anything, Scripture equips us to think as widely as possible and still be secure.

I'm always amused after I make a bold statement, that people will comment, "Well, I wouldn't say what you just said."

I smile and say, "God doesn't know your thoughts, does he?"

They're acting as if God knows only what he hears — in English. They're afraid to verbalize their thoughts for fear God won't like it.

God knows our thoughts, good and bad, creative and trite, spoken and silent. He is entirely in favor of our thinking freely about his world and our particular place in it. These flights of imagination are not frivolous. They are essential to survive.

THREE

LISTENING TO THE LISTENERS

If you preach the gospel in all aspects with the exception of the issues which deal specifically with your time, you are not preaching the gospel at all.

MARTIN LUTHER

Preach to the suffering, and you will never lack a congregation. There is a broken heart in every pew.

JOSEPH PARKER

How do preachers know if they are even communicating, much less convincing?

After *the sermon is too late. The clipped-or-effusive-comment test at the sanctuary door only grades a completed sermon. Nothing more can be done for it.*

Haddon Robinson feels that feedback can begin even "as the sermon is still brewing." The power of persuasion increases when the preacher constructs a sermon for an intimately known congregation. And knowing comes from actively listening to the opinions and passions of the parish.

In the following chapter, Robinson, president of Denver Conservative Baptist Seminary and a convincing preacher in his own right, explores some of the ways to exegete the congregation with the same effectiveness as the text.

What do you think of ser-
mons?" the Institute for Advanced Pastoral Studies asked
churchgoers — and got an earful. Sample responses:
  "Too much analysis and too little answer."
  "Too impersonal, too propositional — they relate nothing to life."
  "Most sermons resemble hovercrafts skimming over the
water on blasts of hot air, never landing anyplace!"
  No wonder sermons are occasionally mocked as "the fine
art of talking in someone else's sleep." Communication
experts dismiss them as "religious monologues." Communication flows best on two-way streets, they argue, while preaching moves in only one direction. And because congregations
can't talk back to register doubts, disagreements, or opinions,
many sermons hit dead ends.
  A second rap is that most ministers overcommunicate.
They feed new concepts and duties to their congregations
before previous ideas can be digested and absorbed. Content
keeps coming, and when frustrated listeners can't keep up
with the conveyor belt, they stop listening.
  Yet monologues afflict the clergy like a genetic disease.

Experiments with dialogue sermons, in vogue a few years ago, have gone the way of the CB radio. What is more, those trained in theological seminaries, where content is king, succumb to the empty-jug fallacy. Getting ideas into someone else's head is akin to filling a jug with water. Preachers invest large segments of time gathering water from books, commentaries, and old class notes but seldom consider time spent with people a valuable resource. While they often possess the gift, knowledge, and fiery enthusiasm, their sermons sound like "manualese" — textbook exegesis. The empty-jug fallacy is summed up in a bit of doggerel:

Cram it in, jam it in;
People's heads are hollow.
Take it in, pour it in;
There is more to follow.

Heads are neither open nor hollow. Heads have lids, screwed on tightly, and no amount of pouring can force ideas inside. Minds open only when their owners sense a need to open them. Even then, ideas must still filter through layers of experience, habit, prejudice, fear, and suspicion. If ideas make it through at all, it's because feedback operates between speaker and listener.

In recent years, auto makers have begun outfitting some models with fuel efficiency gauges to let drivers know how their habits affect consumption. Whenever you stomp on the accelerator, the needle plummets; whenever you drive gently, the indicator rises. Very quickly this feedback helps pinpoint wasteful actions.

Preaching seems to be a zero-feedback situation, a monologue with no return. It does not have to be so. The pull toward monologues can be broken. In fact, significant preaching has always involved dialogue. The most astute preachers allow their eyes and ears to program their mouths. As they stand in the pulpit, they respond to cues from the audience telling them how they are doing. As they prepare, they study not only content but also people, hearing the spoken and unspoken questions. After speaking, they listen intently to find out how they have done.

Most people do not realize that important feedback takes place during the act of preaching. Listening seems passive, a typical Sunday spectator sport. Yet able communicators listen with their eyes. They know that audiences show by their expressions and posture when they understand, approve, question, or are confused. People nod agreement, smile, check their watches, or slump in their seats. Great preachers do not build strong churches nearly as often as great churches through their feedback make strong preachers. These congregations give their preachers the home court advantage by actively listening to what they have to say.

Feedback, however, begins as the sermon is still brewing. Here pastors hold an advantage over other speakers, since they interact daily with members of the audience. Yet this advantage is not automatic. To benefit, preachers must listen: to questions people ask, and for answers they seek. They must observe: needs (expressed or unexpressed, admitted or denied), relationships (personal, family, community), experiences, attitudes, and interests. Jotting down what they observe each day will help them remember the passing parade. This in turn colors and shapes the handling of biblical material and the approach to the message. Let a preacher take a truth from Scripture and force himself to find twenty-five illustrations of that truth in daily life, and he will discover how much the world and its citizens have to tell him.

This dialogue with the congregation and the wider community can be more focused. In order to develop a sensitivity to current questions, John Stott, the internationally known English minister, joined a reading group that met monthly. They explored the ideas and implications of significant books, usually secular, from a Christian perspective. At times they attended films or plays together and then returned to the church to discuss what they had seen.

When Stott preached on contemporary issues, he formed

an ad hoc group of specialists to help him learn the personal dimensions of the problem. At some of these gatherings, Stott actively participated, while at others he merely sat and eavesdropped on discussions between different points of thought. As an outgrowth of the challenging dialogue, Stott's sermons, while solidly biblical, were as up-to-date as next week's news magazine.

Pastors in smaller churches legitimately object that such groups develop more easily in large urban or suburban congregations. Yet even in rural and inner-city communities, men and women wrestle with substantive issues, and many would welcome the opportunity to discuss contemporary life and thought with a minister.

Churches, large or small, can organize systems of feedback. A church in Iowa turns monologue to dialogue by basing its midweek Bible study on the passage for the *following* Sunday's sermon. The pastor provides notes explaining the text, and then the people divide into small groups to explore further meanings and implications for themselves. Out of this encounter, the pastor zeroes in on terms, ideas, and issues he must address and, as an added benefit, often finds illustrations and applications for his sermon. Surprisingly, everyone agrees studying the passage beforehand heightens rather than diminishes interest in the sermon. They are made aware of the biblical material, and they become curious about how the preacher will handle it.

A pastor of a small church in Oregon goes over his sermon with members of his board every Thursday at breakfast. Everyone reads the passage beforehand, and the minister takes a few moments to sketch the broad outline of his message. During the discussion that follows, each shares what the passage says and what it might mean to the congregation. While the minister prepares the sermon, he does not do so in solitary confinement; instead he benefits from the insights and experiences of others in the body of Christ.

Rehearsing the sermon aloud also offers opportunity for feedback. John Wesley read some of his sermons to an uneducated servant girl with the instructions, "If I use a word or phrase you do not understand, you are to stop me." By this exercise, the learned Methodist developed the language of the mines and marketplace.

Many preachers have taken the lead from Wesley. Some have risked their marriages by practicing on their wives. Since preachers' wives marry "for better or for worse," they can cut their downside risks by offering constructive criticism. At Denver Seminary we offer courses to equip wives in making their husbands' sermons better. Less courageous ministers — or those with weaker marriages — might run through their sermons with a shut-in or a friend willing to contribute an ear.

As people file out of the sanctuary on Sunday, they mumble appropriate clichés: "You preached a good sermon today" or "I enjoyed what you had to say." While these responses are nice, they are often little more than code words to get past the minister as he guards the door. Preachers need an *organized* program of feedback following the sermon to determine whether they have hit their target.

Oak Cliff Bible Fellowship in Dallas, Texas, devotes the last fifteen minutes of the service to questions and answers. Some sermons raise more questions than others, of course. When questions are few, members tell what the sermon could mean in their lives. Both questions and testimony not only benefit the people but provide immediate information to the pastor.

According to Reuel Howe, feedback sessions are more productive if the minister is not present. In his book *Partners in Preaching*, Howe suggests inviting six or more lay people, including a couple of teenagers, to take part in a reaction group following the church service. The pastor does not attend, but the conversation is recorded. When the tape runs out, the session ends. That pastor listens to the recorded comments later in the week. Several questions structure interaction.

1. *What did the sermon say to you?*

2. *What difference, if any, do you think the sermon will make in your life?*

3. *How did the preacher's method, language, illustrations, and delivery help or hinder your hearing of the message?*

4. *Do you disagree with any of it? What would you have said about the subject?*

Lay people find these opportunities stimulating. In fact, through them, many learn to listen to sermons more perceptively and develop a keener appreciation of good preaching. If the minister listens carefully, he will discover how his congregation responded, what they heard and did not hear, what they understood and did not understand.

However it comes about, feedback is the lifeblood of communication. Without it, preaching seldom touches life.

When the church was young, Christians gathered at a common meal for Communion and communication. As a teacher explained the Scriptures, listeners broke in with questions and comments. So lively was the feedback that New Testament writers like Paul wrote ground rules to keep this interchange under control. Later, as Christianity fell under the influence of Greek and Roman rhetoric, oratory replaced conversation, and dialogues became monologues.

The infant church possessed what the modern church must rediscover. Only as we talk with people — not at them — will preaching remain a vital and effective carrier of God's truth.

FOUR

ZEAL VS. ART: THE PREACHER'S DILEMMA

The young preacher has been taught to lay out all his strengths on the form, taste, and beauty of his sermon as a mechanical and intellectual product. We have thereby cultivated a vicious taste among the people and raised the clamor for talent instead of grace, eloquence instead of piety, rhetoric instead of revelation, reputation and brilliancy instead of holiness.

E. M. BOUNDS

If conviction is the goal of preaching, what are the legitimate and effective means to that end?

Abraham Lincoln said, "When I hear a man preach, I like to see him act as if he were fighting bees." Exuberance has its attractions, but zealous preaching also packs liabilities. Flailing limbs may so dominate the pulpit that the preacher's zeal upstages the sermon's intent.

On the other hand, pastors able to weave a literate spell with smooth oratory want to do more than impress a receptive crowd. The art of preaching is not intended to displace the aim: hearts moved to believe in Christ and follow his ways.

According to Calvin Miller, combining zeal, art, and results is no recent quandary. Even Old Testament prophets faced the dilemma. Miller, pastor of Westside Baptist Church in Omaha and a popular author, strives to make both art and zeal serve his preaching and writing purposes.

T

he Book of Jonah is the tale of a reluctant preacher. Jonah's message, as we have come to know it, is: "Yet forty days, and Nineveh shall be overthrown" (Jon. 3:4).

A brief eight words. Surely there is more: some clever and imaginative introduction lost in the oral manuscript. There must have been iterations, poetry, and exegesis. But they are gone, and those eight words are all we know.

Such a miniature message seems anticlimactic. Even the king of Nineveh had more to say than Jonah (see vv. 7–9). But the lost sermon was preached and bore a stern word of necessity. Verse 10 states its effect: "And God saw their works, that they turned from their evil way; and God repented of the evil that he had said that he would do unto them; and he did it not."

The results of sermons in the Bible seem to be of great importance. This is true of either Testament. Acts 2:40–41 speaks of the dramatic results of Peter's Pentecostal sermon, and a few days later we are told, "Howbeit many of them which heard the word believed; and the number of the men was about five thousand" (Acts 4:4). While Jonah omits the statistics of his sermon, Luke was careful to note Simon's.

Preaching in the New Testament seems to emulate the authoritative style of the Old Testament prophets. Ever cloaked in other-worldly authority, preaching became the vehicle the early church rode into the arena of evangelizing the Roman Empire. As common people of Galilee once marveled at Christ's authority in the Sermon on the Mount (Matt. 7:28–29), so the authority of Scripture-based sermons became the defense — sometimes the sole defense — of the men and women who pressed the strong alternative of the gospel.

No Time to Waste

From John the Baptist to the end of the New Testament era, the sermon, like the church itself, flamed with apocalyptic zeal. The prophets had preached strong declarations of the direction of God in history. Following Pentecost, the sermon was possessed of a new spiritual union, where the preacher and the Holy Spirit were joined. The sermon, like Scripture, was breathed by the Spirit. Because of a direct alliance with the Trinity, the preacher had the right to speak with God's authority, demanding immediate action and visible decisions. This "right-now" ethic saw the sermon in terms of the demand of God. When God demanded decisions, they could be tabulated as soon as the sermon was finished. Sheep could immediately be divided from goats.

The specific message was delivered by those who possessed the call. The rules of primitive homiletics were not defined. The sermon was the man; the medium, the message. The product was instant and visible. Faith could be tabulated by those who cried in the streets — when they saw their hearers accept the message, submit to baptism, and show up for the breaking of bread and prayers.

Following the first head counts in Jerusalem, the fire of evangelism spread, pushed on by the hot winds of Greek and Aramaic sermons. Congregations sprang up as sermons called them into being. Without institutional structure, programs, or buildings, the church celebrated the simple center of worship — the sermon and that which the sermon created: the company of the committed, the fellowship of believers.

The sermon was not celebrated as art, though doubtless, art may have been an aspect of delivery. Art was not so important in the panicky apocalypticism of Century One. Zeal, not art, raged in the bright light of Pentecost. The sermon was the means of reaching the last, desperate age of humanity. One needed not to polish phrases or study word roots — the kingdom was at hand, and there wasn't time to break ground for a seminary. Church administration went begging. On the eve of Armageddon, committees and bureaus were unimportant. There was only one point to be made. All human wisdom was one set of alternatives: Repent or perish.

This was also Jonah's sermon: Repent or perish. Like those of the New Testament era, his was not a notable document. The sermon was the workhorse of urgent evangelism.

Jonah's sermon was powerful simply because it was not ornate. He who cries "Fire!" in a theater need not be an orator. Indeed, he is allowed to interrupt the art of actors. It is not an offense to the years of disciplined training to be set aside for the urgent and unadorned word: "The theater is on fire!" The bearer rates his effectiveness on how fast the theater is cleared, not on the ovation of the customers. The alarmist is not out for encores but empty seats. His business is rescue.

The Book of Jonah concerns such reluctant and apocalyptic preaching. The royal family sitting at last in the ashes of national repentance illustrates how effective his urgency was.

This zealous declaration is the Word of God as it is preached today in growing churches. Those who would speak an artistic word must do it in churches already built. Further, those who admire the Fosdicks and Maclarens — and they are to be admired — must see that their artistry would be passed by in the slums of London, where Booth's drums and horns sounded not a "trumpet voluntary" to call men and women to the queen's chapel but the "oom-pah-pah" of the cross. "Are you washed in the blood of the Lamb?" was an urgent question that nauseated Anglicans even as it intrigued the poor and downtrodden of England with its zealous demands.

What did Booth say? Who knows? Who cares?

What did Whitefield say? What Billy Sunday? What Finney, what Wesley, what Mordecai Ham? To be sure, some of their sermons survive. But essentially they viewed their preaching not in the Chrysostom tradition but the tradition of the Baptizer of Christ: "O generation of vipers, who hath warned you to flee from the wrath to come? Bring forth therefore fruits worthy of repentance" (Luke 3:7–8), or Simon Peter, who cried, "Save yourselves from this untoward generation" (Acts 2:40).

The Coming of Art

Here and there were men like Jonathan Edwards who combined the best of literary tradition and apocalyptic zeal. But there was a real sense in which Edwards, the Mathers, and the other Puritans supplied a pre-soap-opera generation with a cultural center. The better their apocalypse, the higher the other-world fever of their gospel contagion. Their fiery tirades began to resemble the spirits of a matador, and the amens were the enthusiastic olés, where the champion was not Jehovah but the preacher. Kate Caffrey writes in *The Mayflower*:

> A strong style was favored — in 1642 John Cotton recommended preaching after the manner of Christ, who, he said, "let fly poynt blanck" — and the hearers judged each performance like professional drama critics. Two sermons on Sunday and a lecture-sermon or weeknight meeting, usually on Thursday, were the custom, with fines of up to five shillings for absence from church. Only those who wished need go to the weeknight sermon, which was accompanied by no prayers or other teaching. Yet they were so popular in the sixteen-thirties that the General Court of Massachusetts tried to make every community hold them on the same day, to cut down all the running about

from one town to the next. The preachers protested that it was in order to hear sermons that people had come to New England, so the court contented itself with the mild recommendation that listeners should at least be able to get home before dark.

Even condemned criminals joined in the vogue for sermons. On March 11, 1686, when James Morgan was executed in Boston, three sermons were preached to him by Cotton and Increase Mather and Joshua Moody (so many came to hear Moody that their combined weight cracked the church gallery), and the prisoner delivered from the scaffold a stern warning to all present to take heed from his dread example.

Sermons were so important that it is impossible to overestimate them. Hourglasses, set up by the minister, showed the sermons' length: a bare hour was not good enough. People brought paper and inkhorns to take copious notes in a specially invented shorthand; many thick notebooks filled with closely written sermon summaries have been preserved. The meeting house rustled with the turning of pages and scratching of pens. Sermons were as pervasive then as political news today; they were read and discussed more eagerly than newspapers are now.

These intellectualized, zealous Massachusetts Bay sermons were celebrated by sermon lovers throughout New England. In these meetinghouses the sermon grew in performance value. And yet the zeal and urgency were viewed as part of the performance.

The tendency remains. Now the zealot is a performer and the sermon a monologue celebrated for its emotional and statistical success. The burden is urgent but also entertaining. The preacher feels the burden of his word as the fire-crier feels the pain of his office. But he feels also the pleasure of its success, which is his reputation.

Ego being the force it is, the urgency of the cry often becomes a secondary theme. Artistry eclipses zeal.

In *Moby Dick*, Herman Melville tells us of Father Mapple's sermon on the Book of Jonah. Listen to Mapple's artistic treatment:

Then God spake unto the fish; and from the shuddering cold and blackness of the sea, the whale came breeching up towards the warm and pleasant sun, and all the delights of air and earth; and 'vomited out Jonah upon the dry land'; when the word of the Lord came a second time; and Jonah, bruised and beaten — his ears like two sea-shells, still multitudinously murmuring of the ocean — Jonah did the Almighty's bidding. And what was that, shipmates? To preach the truth to the face of Falsehood! That was it!

This, shipmates, this is that other lesson; and woe to that pilot of the living God who slights it. Woe to him whom this world charms from Gospel duty! Woe to him who seeks to pour oil upon the waters when God has brewed them into a gale! Woe to him who seeks to please rather than to appall! Woe to him whose good name is more to him than goodness! Woe to him who, in this world, courts not dishonour! Yea, woe to him who, as the great Pilot Paul has it, while preaching to others is himself a castaway!

But perhaps Father Mapple's art can afford to be more obvious than his zeal: he is preaching in a church already there and is not delivering urgency but *a sermon on urgency!*

How Shall We Then Preach?

For years I have felt myself trapped in this quandary. Growing a church causes me to speak of redemption, frequently and earnestly. My sermons often sound to me too Falwellian or Criswellian or Pattersonian, my sermons more zealous than artistic. It is their intent to draw persons to Christ, in which pursuit my church is engaged.

But you may object, "Is it only the sermon that builds your church? Do you not use the manuals and conventional machinery of the church and parachurch?" Yes. There have been mailing programs, and such radio and newspaper ads as we could manage. In fact, has not the sermon become second place in the church? Bill Hull once said in a denominational symposium:

Let us candidly confront this chilling claim that the pulpit is no longer the prow of the church, much less of civilization, as Herman Melville visualized it in *Moby Dick*. Ask any pulpit committee after months of intensive investigation and travel: How many pastors in the Southern Baptist Convention are even trying to build their careers on the centrality of preaching? . . . Subtle but excruciating pressures are brought to bear on the minister today to spend all of the week feverishly engineering some spectacular scheme designed to draw attention to his church, then on Saturday night to dust off somebody else's clever sermon outline (semantic gimmickry) for use the next morning.

Is this not so? To some degree, I think it is.

But there are some of us who don't want it to be. We feel called to do the work of an evangelist and believe urgency can have some class and be done with some artistry and/or enlightenment. For years I have listened to the sermons of Richard Jackson, pastor at North Phoenix Baptist Church, with great debt to his example. After he finished a long series on the Passion passage of Saint John, I had seen the Cross in a new light. During more than a year of sermons from that Gospel, more than six hundred were added to his church by baptism. Perhaps Pastor Jackson has taken the burden of urgency to the Greek New Testament and the credible commentators and has emerged to say, "Here is enlightened urgency."

Perhaps Swindoll has done it with certainty. Perhaps Draper did it with Hebrews in his commentary. The sermon by each of these, I believe, is a declaration of urgency that at the same time takes giant strides toward homiletic finesse.

A secular parallel commends itself, again noticed by Bill Hull:

With disaster staring him in the face, Churchill took up the weapon of his adversary and began to do battle with words. From a concrete bomb shelter deep underground, he spoke to the people of Britain not of superiority but of sacrifice, not of conquest but of courage, not of revenge but of renewal. Slowly but surely, Winston Churchill talked England back to life. To beleaguered old men waiting on their rooftops with the buckets of water for the fire bombs to land, to frightened women and children huddled behind sandbags with sirens screaming overhead, to exhausted pilots dodging tracer bullets in the midnight sky, his words not only announced a new dawn but also conveyed the strength to bring it to pass.

No wonder Ruskin described a sermon as "thirty minutes to raise the dead." That is our awesome assignment: to put into words, in such a way that our hearers will put into deeds, the new day that is ours in Jesus Christ our Lord.

I am not talking about dogmatism. Dogmatism is authority-sclerosis. It is an incessant filibuster — never mute, always deaf! Talking is easier and much louder than thinking. The growing church too often cannot celebrate new truth, for it is too long screaming the old ones. The familiar is the creed, the unfamiliar is liberalism and dangerous revisionism. The thinking person off the street may want to ask questions and enter into dialogue, but he finds that trying to ask a question is like shouting into the gale or trying to quote the flag salute at a rock concert. His need for reasons seems buried in the noise.

I have always applauded Huck Finn for deciding to go with Tom Sawyer to hell than with the fundamentalist Miss Watson to heaven:

> Then she told me all about the bad place, and I said I wished I was there. She got mad, then, but I didn't mean no harm. All I wanted was to go somewheres; all I wanted was a change, I wasn't particular. She said it was wicked to say what I said; said she wouldn't say it for the whole world; she was going to live so as to go to the good place. Well, I couldn't see no advantage in going where she was going, so I made up my mind I wouldn't try for it. But I never said so, because it would only make trouble and wouldn't do no good.
>
> Now she had got a start, and she went on and told me all about the good place. She said all a body would have to do there was to

go around all day long with a harp and sing, forever and ever. So I didn't think much of it. But I never said so. I asked her if she reckoned Tom Sawyer would go there, and, she said, not by a considerable sight. I was glad about that, because I wanted him and me to be together.

The logic of the streets is doubly plagued by such images. Why would a robust, open-minded Christ so love an over-corseted, dispeptic, neurotic Scripture quoter as Miss Watson? Hell, for all its fiery disadvantages, seems a quieter and kinder place than her heaven.

It is not that saying "Thus saith the Lord" is wrong, and yet we are all drawn by the counsel of a friend who says, "Let us look together at what the Lord saith"! When we become more authoritarian in dialogues, we need to be sure we are really speaking the mind of God and not merely strong-arming our own agenda in another's more mighty name.

What Matters Most

Still, as crass as it sounds, unless the preached word encounters and changes its hearers in some way, artistry and enchantment cannot be said to have mattered much. The sermon must not at last be cute, but life changing. As Somerset Maugham said of certain writers, "Their flashy effects distract the mind. They destroy their persuasiveness; you would not believe a man was very intent on ploughing a furrow if he carried a hoop with him and jumped through it at every other step."

When the sermon has reasoned, exhorted, pled, and pontificated; when it has glittered with art and oozed with intrigue; when it has entered into human hearts and broken secular thralldom — when all of this has been done, the sermon must enter into judgment at a high tribunal. Like the speaker who uttered it, the sermon must hear the judgment of the last great auditor. If, indeed, every word is brought to God, one can imagine the last great gathering of the sermons of all ages — the MARCH OF THE CASSETTES PAST THE THRONE. Every word tried . . . a thousand, thousand sermons — indeed, a great multitude which no man could number: Peter Marshall, Peter the Hermit, Peter the Apostle, Peter Piper, Peter Paul, Popes, Carl McIntire, Oral Roberts, Robert Bellarmine, John R. Rice, John Newton, John Hus, Prince John — a thousand, thousand words from David Brainerd to Origen, Tertullian to Swaggart, Jack Van Impe to Arius, all at once replying to one issue: Which sermons really counted?

The God who is the ancient lover of sinners will cry to those sermons at his left hand, "Why did you not serve me? Why did you not love men and women enough to change them? You took their hearts, commanded their attention, but did nothing to change them. Be gone, ye cursed sermons, to Gehenna — be burned to ashes and scattered over chaos — for better sermons would have called chaos to unfold itself in strong creation."

Part II
PROCLAIMING

F I V E
HOW TO DECLARE THE GOSPEL

When I begin my sermons I dare the person not to listen to me. Not that I'm that great — it's just that I've got something to say that's too important to ignore.

CHARLES SWINDOLL

If it were only texts or men we had to handle! But we have to handle the gospel.

P. T. FORSYTH

Preaching right is a little like dressing right: You have to know what goes with what. Most pastors learn early on not to wear a paisley tie with a plaid shirt or white bucks with gray pinstripes.

In the following chapter, Aurelius Augustine instructs preachers to dress their speech appropriately if they will declare the gospel with convincing results.

But how does one fashion a sermon for the circumstances? When should a preacher shout, when plead, when whisper, when reason? Augustine ventures different styles — the temperate and the majestic — and proposes occasions for their use. He suggests the language to use and the effects to seek. For instance, in dissuading civil war in Mauritania, he knew applause counted little; only a deeper response signaled conviction.

Augustine, one of the ancient church's greatest theologians, served as bishop of Hippo in a pagan North African culture from A.D. 395 until his death in 430. His two most famous works, Confessions *and* The City of God, *have become classics of Christian literature.*

Augustine wrote in Latin, and most English translations date from the late eighteen hundreds. So we've tried to update the language where appropriate in order to make your reading easier. If you stay with the chapter, we think you'll find this excerpt from On Christian Doctrine *has timeless application to the task of preaching to convince.*

The teacher of Holy Scripture must teach what is right and refute what is wrong. In doing this, he must conciliate the hostile, rouse the careless, and tell the ignorant about current events and trends for the future. Once his hearers are friendly, attentive, and ready to learn (whether he has found them so or he has made them so), the teacher uses three methods to communicate truth:

- If the hearers need teaching, tell the truth by means of narrative.
- If the hearers need doubtful points cleared up, use reasoning and exhibition of proofs.
- If the hearers need to be roused rather than instructed, vigorous speech is needed. Here entreaties, reproaches, exhortations, upbraidings, and all the other means of rousing the emotions are necessary.

All these methods are constantly used by nearly everyone engaged in teaching. Some teachers employ them coarsely, inelegantly, and frigidly, while others use them with acuteness, elegance, and spirit. Both kinds can be effective. But a teacher should be able to argue and speak with wisdom, if not with eloquence, and with profit to his hearers (even though he profits them less than if he could speak with eloquence too).

Always beware, however, of the man who abounds in eloquent nonsense, especially if the hearer is pleased with worthless oratory and thinks that because the speaker is eloquent what he says must be true. As that great teacher of rhetoric, Cicero, rightly said, "Although wisdom without eloquence is often of little service, eloquence without wisdom does positive injury, and is never of service."

One caution: some passages are misunderstood no matter how clearly the speaker may expound them. These should never be brought before the people at all, or only on rare occasions when there is some urgent reason. In those situations two conditions are to be insisted upon: our hearers should have an earnest desire to learn the truth and should have the capacity of mind to receive it in whatever form it may be communicated.

The Necessity of a Lucid Style

A desire for clearness sometimes leads to neglect of polished speech. One author, when dealing with speech of this kind, says that there is in it "a kind of careful negligence."

Of course, we agree that the highest priority should be placed on clarity. What advantage is there in speech that does not lead to understanding? Therefore, good teachers avoid all words that do not teach; instead they must find words that are both pure and intelligible.

This is true not only in personal conversations but much more in the case of public speech. In conversation anyone has the power of asking a question; but in an oration all faces are turned upon the speaker, and it is neither customary nor decorous for a person to ask a question about what he does not understand. On this account the speaker ought to be especially careful to give assistance to those who cannot ask it.

How can one tell if further explanation is needed? A crowd anxious for instruction generally shows by its movement if it understands. Until some indication of this sort is given, the teacher should discuss the subject over and over, and put it in every shape and form and variety of expression. As soon, however, as the speaker has determined that he is understood, he ought either to end his address or pass on to another point.

Speak Clearly but Not Inelegantly

True eloquence consists not in making people like what they disliked, nor in making them do what they shrank from, but in making clear what was obscure. Yet if this is done without grace of style, the benefit does not extend beyond the few eager students who learn no matter how unpolished the form of the teaching. There is an analogy between learning and eating: the very food without which it is impossible to live must be flavored to meet the tastes of the majority.

Accordingly, Cicero has said, "An eloquent man must speak so as to teach, to delight, and to persuade." Then he adds: "To teach is a necessity, to delight is a beauty, to persuade is a triumph." Now of these three, the first (teaching) depends on what we say, the other two on the way we say it.

For the fastidious (those who care not for truth unless it is put in the form of a pleasing discourse), a superior teacher must learn the art of pleasing. And yet even this is not enough for those stubborn-minded men who both understand and are pleased with the teacher's discourse but derive no profit from it. For what does it profit a man if he both confesses the truth and praises the eloquence, yet does not yield his consent?

We need to say here that some truths need only be believed. To give one's assent implies nothing more than to confess that they are true. Some truths, however, must be put into practice and are taught for the very purpose of being practiced. It is useless to be intellectually persuaded of those truths (and, indeed, to be pleased with the beauty of their expression) if they are not learned to be practiced.

Using the Right Style

Although teachers of biblical truth are speaking of great matters, they should not always use a majestic tone. When instructing, they should use a subdued tone. When giving praise or blame, a temperate tone is appropriate. When, however, the teaching calls for action, we must speak with power in a manner calculated to sway the mind. Sometimes the same important matter is treated in all these ways at different times: quietly when being taught, temperately when its importance is being urged, and powerfully when we are forcing a mind adverse to the truth to turn and embrace it.

For example, there is nothing greater than God himself. Yet teaching the doctrine of the Trinity calls for calm discussion. It is a subject difficult to comprehend, and our goal is mainly to understand as much as possible.

But when we come to praise God, what a field for beauty and splendor of language opens up before us! Who can exhaust his powers to the utmost in praising him whom no one can adequately praise?

And if we are challenging our hearers to worship God, then we ought to speak out with power and impressiveness, to show how great an honor this is.

We have many examples of the three styles right in Scripture. We have an example of the calm, *subdued style* in the apostle Paul, where he says:

> My brothers, I am going to use an everyday example: when two people agree on a matter and sign an agreement, no one can break it or add anything to it. Now, God made his promises to Abraham and to his descendant. The Scripture does not use the plural "descendants," meaning many people, but the singular "descendant," meaning one person only, namely, Christ. What I mean is that God made a covenant with Abraham and promised to keep it. The Law, which was given four hundred and thirty years later, cannot break that covenant and cancel God's promise. For if God's gift depends on the Law, then it no longer depends on this promise. However, it was because of his promise that God gave that gift to Abraham. (Gal. 3:15–18)

And because it might possibly occur to the hearer to ask, "If there is no inheritance by the Law, why then was the Law given?" Paul himself anticipates this objection and asks, "What, then, was the purpose of the Law?" And he answers his own question:

> It was added to show what wrongdoing is, and it was meant to last until the coming of Abraham's descendant, to whom the promise was made. The Law was handed down by angels, with a man acting as a go-between. But a go-between is not needed when only one person is involved; and God is one. (Gal. 3:19–20)

In the following words of the apostle, we have the *temperate style:* "Do not rebuke an older man, but appeal to him as if he were your father. Treat the younger men as your brothers, the older women as mothers, and the younger women as sisters, with all purity" (1 Tim. 5:1–2). And also in these: "So then, my brothers, because of God's great mercy to us I appeal to you: Offer yourselves as a living sacrifice to God, dedicated to his service and pleasing to him. This is the true worship that you should offer" (Rom. 12:1). Almost the whole of this passage in Romans is exhortation in the temperate style of eloquence.

The *majestic style* of speech differs from the temperate style chiefly in that it is not so much decked out with verbal ornaments as exalted by mental emotion. It uses nearly all the ornaments that the temperate does but without needing them as much. For it is borne along by its own energy; the force of the thought, not the ornamentation, makes the real impact.

The apostle in the following passage is urging that for the sake of ministry we should patiently bear all the evils of life. It is a great subject treated with power, and the ornaments of speech are not wanting.

> In our work together with God, then, we beg you who have received God's grace not to let it be wasted. Hear what God says:
> "When the time came for me to show you favor,
> I heard you;
> when the day arrived for me to save you,
> I helped you."

Listen! This is the hour to receive God's favor; today is the day to be saved!

We do not want anyone to find fault with our work, so we try not to put obstacles in anyone's way. Instead, in everything we do we show that we are God's servants by patiently enduring troubles, hardships, and difficulties. We have been beaten, jailed, and mobbed; we have been overworked and have gone without sleep or food. By our purity, knowledge, patience, and kindness we have shown ourselves to be God's servants — by the Holy Spirit, by our true love, by our message of truth, and by the power of God. We have righteousness as our weapon, both to attack and to defend ourselves. We are honored and disgraced; we are insulted and praised. We are treated as liars, yet we speak the truth; as unknown, yet we are known by all; as though we were dead, but as you see, we live on. Although punished, we are not killed; although saddened, we are always glad; we seem poor, but we make many people rich; we seem to have nothing, yet we really possess everything.

Dear friends in Corinth! We have spoken frankly to you; we have opened our hearts wide. It is not we who have closed our hearts to you; it is you who have closed your hearts to us. I speak now as though you were my children: show us the same feelings that we have for you. Open your hearts wide! (2 Cor. 6:1–13)

The Necessity of Variety

It is not against the rules to mingle these various styles. Although in most speeches one style will predominate, every variety of style should be used, consistent with good taste. For when we keep monotonously to one style, we fail to retain the hearer's attention. But when we move from one style to another, the discourse has more grace even though it tends to last longer.

Each style has distinctives that prevent the hearer's attention from cooling. We can bear the subdued style, however, longer without variety than the majestic style. The mental emotion necessary to stimulate the hearer's feelings can be maintained only a short time. Therefore we must avoid trying to carry the emotional pitch too high or too long, lest we lose what we have already gained.

Mingling the Various Styles

Now it is important to determine what style should be alternated with what other, and the places where any particular style should be used. In the majestic style, for instance, it is almost always desirable that the introduction should be temperate. And the speaker has it in his discretion to use the subdued style even where the majestic would be allowable, in order that the majestic, when it *is* used, may be the more majestic by comparison.

Further, whatever may be the style of the speech or writing, when knotty questions turn up for solution, the subdued style is naturally demanded. And we must use the temperate style whenever praise or blame is to be given, no matter what may be the general tone of the discourse.

In the majestic style, then, and also in the subdued, both the other two styles occasionally find a place. The temperate style, on the other hand, occasionally needs the quiet style. But the temperate style never needs the aid of the majestic, for its object is to gratify, not excite, the mind.

If frequent and vehement applause follows a speaker, do not suppose that only the majestic style has been used. This effect is often produced both by the accurate distinctions of the quiet style and by the beauties of the temperate. The majestic style, on the other, frequently silences the audience by its impressiveness and calls forth their tears.

For example, when at Caesarea in Mauritania I was dissuading the people from that civil, or worse than civil, war they called Caterva (for it was not fellow citizens merely, but neighbors, brothers, fathers, and sons even, who, divided into two factions and armed with stones, fought annually at a certain season of the year for several days continuously, everyone killing whomever he could), I strove with all the vehemence of speech I could command to root out and drive from their hearts and lives an evil so cruel. It was not, however, when I heard their applause but when I saw their tears that I thought I had produced an effect. For the applause showed that they were instructed and delighted, but the tears that they were convinced to stop.

Watch and Pray

But whatever may be the eloquence of the style, the life of the speaker will count for more in securing the hearer's compliance. The man who speaks wisely and eloquently but lives wickedly may, it is true, instruct many who are anxious to learn (though, as it is written, he "is unprofitable to himself").

But they would do good to many more if they lived as they preach. For some people seek an excuse for their own evil lives by comparing the teaching with the conduct of their instructors. They say in their hearts or even with their lips, "Why do you not do yourself what you bid me do?" They cease to listen with submission to a man who does not listen to himself, and in despising the preacher they learn to despise the word that is preached. The apostle Paul told Timothy, "Do not let anyone look down on you because you are young, but be an example for the believers in your speech, your conduct, your love, faith, and purity" (1 Tim. 4:12).

And so our Christian teacher, even though he says what is just, holy, and good (and he ought never to say anything else), doing all he can to be heard with intelligence, pleasure, and obedience, will succeed more by piety in prayer than by gifts of oratory. So he ought to pray for himself, and for those he is about to address, before he attempts to speak. When the hour comes to speak, he ought, before he opens his mouth, to lift up his thirsty soul to God, to drink in what he is about to pour forth, and to be himself filled with what he is about to distribute.

Thus the Holy Spirit speaks in those who for Christ's sake are delivered to the persecutors; why not also in the teachers who deliver Christ's message to those who are willing to learn?

SIX

WHY SOME SERMONS WORK BETTER THAN OTHERS

As the nineteenth-century German theologian Tholuck said, "A sermon ought to have heaven for its father and the earth for its mother." But if such sermons are to be born, heaven and earth have to meet in the preacher.

JOHN R. W. STOTT

Billy Graham preaching in an elevator would be a little overwhelming, but Fred Rogers of "Mr. Rogers's Neighborhood" teaching in the Los Angeles Coliseum might tend to underwhelm. The number of listeners determines much about the style of preaching. What flies with one group flops with another.

How you convince a handful differs from how you sway a crowd. Even the optimum content for a sermon will vary with the size of the congregation. Some subjects work best in the give-and-take of a group; others shine in mass meetings. Certain techniques lend themselves to a midsized crowd; others to an intimate setting. Skillful preachers select their subjects and techniques with an eye to the audience.

This is the subject William Kruidenier explores in the following chapter. Kruidenier is pastor of Emmanuel Christian Fellowship in Atlanta, Georgia. His analysis helps put dimensions on an often-perplexing question: Why do some sermons work better than others?

And, even better, he offers suggestions for designing sermons suitable for the various occasions.

On any given Sunday, when-
ever a sermon seems to fall short of what we'd hoped for
(realistically or otherwise), we quickly look for a reason. Our
notes (or manuscript) were flawed. We didn't deliver the
message powerfully enough. We didn't get enough sleep the
night before. The sanctuary was too hot. Or too cool. People
just aren't as hungry for spiritual growth as they should
be. . . .

I think there is another explanation, perhaps more common
than many of the above. It has to do with the *match-up* between the message and the group.

One helpful insight of the past decade is that not all groupings in a church are the same. Thinkers in the area of church
growth have pointed out that when you gather the saints on
Sunday morning, you have a *celebration*. In medium- and
large-size churches, the individuals don't all know each other
personally, but that is not the focus; they are rather caught up
in worshiping God.

Break into groups of anywhere from twenty to a hundred,
and you have a *congregation* — people who know one another
and view themselves as a special band (e.g., a choir, a "mini-

church," a permanent Sunday school class). The fellowship is lively, the relationships mainly horizontal. (Smaller churches maintain this closeness even on Sunday morning, which, in fact, is one of their assets.)

To take a quantum leap in intimacy, however, limit the numbers to ten and call for serious commitment and accountability. This is the *cell*.

A fourth kind of group is the *class*, where people gather not primarily to worship, fellowship, or grow personally, but to learn a new skill or body of information. An elective course on evangelism or the Pentateuch is a good example. The focus is on the content, and any worship or fellowship is a by-product.

Most of us are familiar with this. But only recently, as I've been immersed in the challenge of starting a new church and thinking through its formative structures, have I faced what all this means for homiletics.

Making the Good Match

Each kind of group has its own dynamics. What works in one setting will not necessarily succeed in another. But all too often, I have failed to match my proclamation with the dynamic of my particular audience. I've just stood up and done the single specialty I was taught in seminary: expository preaching.

What happens when parishioners hear expositions of Galatians on Sunday morning, 2 Timothy on Sunday night, and something from the Old Testament midweek, all in the same basic style?

They rarely sense that the pastor's message is for *now* — for this group, this moment in time. They go home with a vague feeling of *If you've heard one sermon, you've heard 'em all*. So why go to another service for more of the same?

Here is another problem. Suppose in the worship (celebration) service, I come to a text that mentions the training of children. From the pulpit I go into detail on techniques of child discipline; I even venture some comments about spanking.

Many young parents who are listening appreciate the information — but go away frustrated because they weren't able to raise their hands and ask follow-up questions. Meanwhile, the nonparents present (middle and older adults, singles) gaze out the window.

Certain types of scriptural truth raise certain needs in an audience that can be met only in certain group settings. That is why I have come to adopt the following guidelines:

Texts Appropriate for the Setting

Before opening the Bible, first ask, "What is the focus of this group?" If celebration, it is God. If congregation, it is social fellowship and kinship in Christ. If cell, it is personal growth and accountability. If class, it is skill or information.

Next question: What portions of Scripture originally spoke to these kinds of needs? Some obvious examples:

The Psalms, Romans 9, parts of the Major Prophets, and others lifted the attention of the original readers to the transcendence of God. Thus they make excellent choices to be expounded in celebration or worship services.

In contrast, much of the Pauline corpus dealt with problems in the Christian community. Proverbs and many of the Minor Prophets also speak to community issues. These can be used to promote the same results in a congregation-sized group today.

For the cell, where personal religion is the focus, books such as James, Proverbs, and the life of Christ from the Gospels are highly appropriate. They concentrate on personally living out the faith. They convict us; they promote self-analysis and confession.

The class works best when a task attitude is established: "We're going to survey Romans," or "Let's learn the best way to do a word study in personal Bible investigation." This is not a license for boring teaching. But it does allow us to speak more technically, less personally than in the other three groups.

Truths Appropriate to the Group

This is not entirely in line with my seminary homiletics classes, which urged me to discover at all costs the main thought of any passage of Scripture (in the mind of the original writer) and then convey that same thought to my listeners. While I was always encouraged to know and read my audiences, I was not taught very effectively how to apply the Scriptures on the basis of what the group dynamic would allow.

Some truths from a passage will connect with a particular group like lightning hitting a radio tower, while others barely sputter over the front edge of the podium. The preacher's task is to select those that will strike hard and fast.

If I am working through the Book of Romans and come to chapter 8, verses 26–30 ("The Spirit helps us in our weakness. . . . We know that in all things God works for the good of those who love him. . . ." etc.), I can emphasize different aspects depending on the group.

Celebration: the sovereignty of God over his creation

Congregation: a lighter, less theological, more humorous treatment, full of instances from my life and others' of how God's sovereignty has worked itself out in daily and family living; a "hang-in-there" message

Cell: a hard look at my personal attitudes and actions when the situation demands that I depend on God's sovereignty; counsel, exhortation, confession, forgiveness, a time of building and healing

Class: here I tackle the thorny subject of predestination from the perspectives of biblical, systematic, and historical theology.

Planning the Appropriate Response

Just as each of the four groupings has a different focus, each is different when it comes to response. The preacher does well to think this through ahead of time.

In the celebration event, my chief end is to bring individuals (both Christians and non-Christians) into contact with a transcendent, personal God. That means they need an opportunity to respond to him in repentance and faith. If I do not provide that before the end of the meeting, it is incomplete.

So there must be ways for non-Christians to meet Christ as Savior and Lord. There must be ways for Christians to repent of waywardness. Some of the methods to accommodate these are invitations, staffed prayer or counseling rooms available at the close, and allowance for individual responses such as hands raised in prayer or praise. These all show that we have not forgotten the goal of a celebration service: to bring men and women into contact with God.

My presentation in such a service is necessarily a lecture (one speaking to many without dialogue). In a congregation-sized group, however, this should never be true. In a true congregation, the people know each other well and have developed the social skills of communicating with one another. This greatly aids the learning process if we take advantage of it. Therefore, we structure to allow discussion, dialogue, and even disagreement, so the body of Christ can hammer out the application of the Word to their lives together.

A well-designed congregation group, over the long run, is probably the most effective evangelism agent among the four types. It lets non-Christians hear and observe a loving community of Christians dialoguing together about Christ and their relationships to him. After the meetings, social interaction over refreshments or a meal lets the Word continue to be a stimulus for discussion.

The structure of a cell meeting must be the most flexible of all, since we never know what personal needs lurk behind the members' masks of contentment. A properly structured cell group gives the Spirit of God freedom to leave the teaching outline after only the first point is covered if it raises a need in someone's life. The cell leader can — and should — say, "Let's pick up here next week," whenever an unforeseen but worthwhile diversion comes along. This is acceptable pedagogy.

The class, of course, cannot just hand out information; it

must discern whether the skill or content is being comprehended. Laboratory practice sessions (for students to use skills) or else quizzes (to measure retained information) must complement the teaching of the Word in a class group.

Specialists for Each Kind of Group

One of the discouragements we pastors bring on ourselves is attempting to excel in all four group situations. We assume that, having completed our training in homiletics, we ought to be consummate communicators at any level of group dynamic in the church.

Not so. Certain personality types and sets of gifts or abilities function much better in certain group situations than in others, and even seminary graduates are not exempt from this fact. We all need help discerning which roles in the body of Christ we might best fill. Then we could benefit from separate training, both exegetical and homiletical, tailored to the group dynamic best suited to us.

Far more lay teachers as well can be trained for local-church effectiveness if we align our training more closely with the needs and focuses of group dynamics.

Beware of Cross-Mixing Techniques

The above discussion is not meant to say that worship can occur only in a celebration service, fellowship in a congregation, growth and accountability in a cell, and instruction and training in a class. But it does say these goals are the easiest to accomplish in the various settings.

There are times when it is good to attempt to worship in a cell, or to encourage one another on Sunday morning. But such mixing should be done intentionally and intelligently, not accidentally. We must understand first what the best setting is for such a practice, and not expect as great a result if we choose to go ahead in a less than optimum context.

The things I have said here about preaching and teaching, like the four group classifications themselves, are not really new. The group dynamics have existed for centuries; only recently have we put names and definitions on them. So also, pastors long before me have sensed instinctively what worked best in one setting or another, and have gone about their ministry accordingly.

What is new here is, I hope, a clearer statement about why they succeeded. If we understand the kinds of groups a church needs to function well and meet the worship, fellowship, intimacy, and instructional needs of its people, and if we grasp how to narrow the focus of the Word of God in those groups to more effectively capitalize on their dynamics, then the net result should be more specific needs in more people's lives being satisfied. And that is what ministry is all about.

S E V E N

RAISINS IN THE OATMEAL: THE ART OF ILLUSTRATING

An illustration is like a row of footlights that shed light on what is presented on the stage. If you turn the lights onto the audience, they blind the people.

HADDON ROBINSON

The greatest convincer preached with stories — a woman's lost coin, treacherous renters, faithful servants. The simple stories communicated to depths that profound propositions would never reach.

Even the gospel itself is a story — a living (and dying and living again) illustration.

What preachers gather and swap and treasure like stamp collectors, they also want to use effectively: their sermon illustrations. But how? How can a preacher know when enough yarns have been spun? At what point does an entertaining illustration bully the text out of the spotlight? When is an illustration demanded? And when does one demean?

Mark Littleton is a Christian communicator who has asked those questions and arrived at some answers — answers he utilized in his former pastorate at Berea Baptist Church in Glen Burnie, Maryland, and answers now used in his writing ministry. Having made the common mistakes and learned from them, he offers his observations in the following chapter.

A

Anyone who must preach two different sermons on Sunday and a third on Wednesday, plus teach, give children's sermons, and offer "a few words" here, there, and everywhere, knows the power of good illustrations. They bring fresh air to musty monologues. They grab the heart as well as the head. They help apply truth to life.

That's why I collect, make up, steal, borrow, and beg them from everyone. My three-by-five card file of illustrations is so cherished I keep a picture of it in my wallet to show friends.

"Get a load of this baby," I say. "Beautiful tan finish, full of laughter and babble, always ready to raise a smile. Everything from anecdotes to zoology. Of course, there are the occasional messes and 2 A.M. feedings, but it's all worth it."

Even more crucial then keeping the box full is the problem of use: How do I match the right illustration with the right situation? Too often we hear a good joke and instantly begin sniffing for a place to tell it. Any time will do, so long as it occurs in next Sunday's sermon. We fall into the pit of depending more on our stories than the power of God's Word and Spirit to hold the listener.

At that point, our illustrations block rather than bring understanding. After all, there is a difference between the *almost right* illustration and the *right* one. As Mark Twain said, "The difference between the right word and the almost right word is the difference between lightning and the lightning bug."

Getting the Right Illustration

Three questions are useful in determining an illustration's efficiency:

Does my point need an illustration? I'm the type who's terrified of being boring, so I've learned to think in analogies and anecdotes. Sometimes I overdo it. If the people understand my point and don't need further clarification, why use up my ammo? No need to shoot dead geese. My temptation is that if I've got a good story, I want to use it now, and if I've got two good stories, quotes, or poems, I want to use them both. (Once I got lost in one point with five illustrations. It was fun but foolish.) Life is too short and sermons too long to heap on the burning coals.

So in preparing a sermon, I simply ask, "When I struggled to understand this idea, did I have to create an illustration to explain it? Did I find myself saying, 'For example . . .'?" This almost always happens when I have something abstract, cerebral, or theological at hand.

Recently in a sermon from Ephesians on "redemption through his blood," I wanted to make the point that not even "good" people are acceptable candidates for heaven on the basis of their goodness. The natural question was "Why not?" All sorts of abstract answers swirled in my head, but I needed to distill the vaporous abstractions into something my size. My mind roamed over all kinds of things — personal experiences, quotes, analogies.

Finally, I remembered a friend's bargain with his children, who resisted eating their vegetables. He and his wife decided to let the kids have one "most-hated" vegetable they would never have to eat. But they had to eat the rest without argument. Mealtimes improved noticeably.

Suppose God gave us all one most-hated commandment

and allowed us to ignore that one in heaven. We would, of course, have to obey the rest. Heaven with people just one law less than perfect would be no better than earth. This analogy made the need for redemption clear to me and, hopefully, to the congregation.

Another way to determine whether a point needs illustrating is to try it out on a friend, spouse, or fellow minister. "Do you understand this point?" If our explanation leaves them cold, start searching for illustrations.

Many times, however, a point is clear, and illustrations only clutter the issue. Often the Bible provides its own word picture to explain the truth. Added ingredients, like day-old manna, can turn wormy and stink, spoiling the impact of an already powerful message.

What is my purpose or goal for this point? What do I want to do with an illustration? Consider some legitimate purposes — and some scriptural examples.

1. To clarify a point — Jesus' parables of the lost coin and sheep.

2. To show a real-life application — much of the Sermon on the Mount.

3. To convict of sin — Nathan's parable to David of the poor man's sheep.

4. To inspire and move to action — the parables of the Prodigal Son and the Good Samaritan.

5. To convince someone of truth — Paul reminding the Athenians of "the unknown god."

6. To make truth memorable — Jesus' unique sayings, such as the camel passing through the eye of a needle.

Pinpointing my purpose helps me see what I want the illustration to accomplish. If I want to convict of sin, I am not going to use a light, inspirational story. I must speak in specific terms of sins people in my congregation may not be aware they are committing. Several times I have confused people by telling something funny in the midst of a serious point, and everyone got off track. A serious illustration would have been much wiser.

What kind of illustration best suits my purpose? To answer this third question, I consult my files, library, friends, and memory for *quantity*. Then I select the best one on the basis of quality. That is one reason I believe in gathering illustrations by the bale. Quantity usually yields quality.

Certain general categories fit certain purposes. For instance, analogies and made-up stores are often excellent to enlighten. Object lessons, anecdotes, cross-references, and word studies are also good.

Sometimes, on the other hand, something light is necessary. In one sermon I wanted to say our world would never have peace until Jesus returned. I knew some people would take a dim view of that. I needed something light but enlightening. I tried a story about a dour Englishman seated on a train between two ladies arguing about the window. One claimed she would die of heat stroke if it weren't opened. The other said she would expire of pneumonia if it didn't stay closed. The ladies called the conductor, who didn't know how to solve the problem. Finally, the gentleman spoke up. "First, open the window. That will kill the one. Then close it. That will kill the other. Then we will have peace." Everyone in the congregation, regardless of political stripe, could appreciate the story.

To move people to action, several ingredients are necessary. First, the proposed action must be clear. That means many quickie examples of how to do what you are asking. Often, this is preceded by "like." "Like when your mother-in-law says . . ." Second, the illustration must end with a clear exhortation. Give an example of a person who responded correctly. People need positive illustrations of what they're to do.

To convict a congregation of something — sin, personal need, lostness — there is a different route: The listener must identify with the illustration. Personal experiences are valuable here as well as situations and roleplays — anything that involves people with the story.

For instance, I wanted my congregation to see the need for trust in God even when they don't know all the hows and whys. I told about my diphtheria/tetanus shot when I was seven years old.

"It won't hurt," the doctor assured me. "Just keep thinking *It's not going to hurt,* and everything will be OK."

But it did hurt. My arm was still sore the next day, and I demanded an explanation from my mother. Why did I have a sore arm?

She couldn't explain the physiological causes of my pain, nor could she explain to my satisfaction how the vaccine could prevent diphtheria. Finally she said, "Mark, I know you don't understand, but you do know I love you, and this shot was something we had to do to protect you."

Because I trusted my mom, I was able to accept the pain.

The people in the congregation could identify — most had experienced the same feelings. Deep inside, they knew the difference between trust and understanding — and that trust sometimes must precede knowledge. But the illustration brought to the surface what they already knew down deep.

In order to convince, an illustration must have authority. Sources with unquestioned authority — scientific reports, research, statistics, quotes from well-known people — may not absolutely prove the point, but most people find them convincing.

Finally, if the purpose is to make a point memorable, other elements are crucial: simplicity, uniqueness, usefulness, truthfulness, and most of all, vividness. An Arab proverb says, "The best speaker is he who turn ears into eyes." In fact, I recall reading that proverb only once, but because of its vividness, it stuck.

Consider some of these memorable expressions that I never tried to memorize but were instantly nailed to my mind. From Haddon Robinson: "A mist in the pulpit is a fog in the pew." Howard Hendricks: "You can't build a skyscraper on a chicken coop foundation." Tony Campolo: "I'm sick and tired of people playing a thousand verses of 'Just as I Am,' who come down just as they are, and go out just as they were."

Using the Right Illustration

Simply placing the right illustration with the right point is not enough. Good preparation includes good declaration. Here are some suggestions for serving illustrations hot.

1. *Don't waste time getting into the story. Get in and get out.* Don't overexplain, apologize, or make other unnecessary comments such as "I found this perfect illustration the other day . . ." Such comments challenge the listener to prove us wrong rather than to wait eagerly for the story.

2. *Make sure the people know what you're illustrating.* Too often they remember the illustration and forget the point. Why? We don't rivet the point to the illustration by repeating it before and after.

3. *Make sure your illustration doesn't overshadow your point.* Many ripping good stories rip up the house and the sermon. All the people get is a good laugh.

4. *Be excited about the illustration.* If I'm not convinced it's interesting and worthwhile, the audience won't be. If I can't generate enthusiasm about the material, I can hardly support it with the luster of a convincing rendition. Rather, I rend it to shreds.

5. *Make sure it's believable and true.* On one occasion, when I had converted a devotional-guide story to first-person, my father remarked, "It sounded bogus to me." Some speakers say that putting yourself into a story, whether you really were there or not, is legitimate. But it can also create distrust. I have heard several well-known preachers use anecdotes I've read in old illustration books. They tell them as though the experience happened to them. Their credibility is destroyed.

6. *Make sure people will identify with the illustration.* Arthur Miller, the playwright, once said that if he came away from a play exclaiming, "That was me!" it was a success. When I see myself in it, that often indicates a potent illustration.

7. *Be sure of your facts.* One night I referred to a book and said the author had died recently. A student in the group nearly shot out of his seat. "Good grief! I just heard him last

week at seminary. You mean he died over the weekend?"

I choked, looked for the door, and confessed, "I think I got the name wrong." Where's the grave? I wanted to crawl in.

8. *Be visual.* Visual speaking creates pictures in the listeners' minds. It uses sharp verbs and nouns, few adjectives. Lots of color and specifics. No fuzzy generalities, just hard slabs of meaning.

Illustrating sermons is one of preaching's most gratifying and challenging tasks. If an illustration is too big for its britches, it tends to break a sermon. If it's too little, the sermon comes across with the clout of a feather. But the *right* illustration, used well, makes preaching not only interesting but effective.

EIGHT
PULPIT PLAGIARISM

In fact, it is as difficult
to appropriate the thoughts
of others as it is to invent.

RALPH WALDO EMERSON

Though old the thought
and oft exprest
'Tis his at last
who says it best.

JAMES RUSSELL LOWELL

A significant part of preaching to convince is the skill of making a sermon breathe life through illustrations. Paul borrowed from philosophers and prophets; Jesus drew heavily from the Old Testament writers. Some were credited and others not. How's a preacher to know where to plant the verbal footnote? And what's fair game to steal — credited or not?

Preachers are rightfully wary of signing their name on another's illustration. No preacher wants to appear phony or unoriginal when worshipers recognize an unnamed source.

Jamie Buckingham, senior minister of Tabernacle Church in Melbourne, Florida, knows the value of the appropriated thought in his preaching and writing. He has also wrestled with the subtle distinction between a pirate and a parrot, between larceny and license.

The following chapter helps preachers draw the ethical distinction in their own sermons, so their illustrations convince their congregations of something greater than their preacher's pilferage.

W hen I bought my Apple IIe Word Processor, I discovered the capabilities of split-screen programming. By pushing the right combination of buttons, I could look at two things simultaneously. The top, for instance, could show data typed in earlier, while the bottom remained blank.

I asked my instructor how this could be useful.

"It is used primarily for plagiarism," he said candidly. "By putting someone else's material on the top screen, you can then rewrite it.

"It's done all the time," he winked.

I thought of the mess Alex Haley got in when he was accused by an obscure writer of having stolen his material — word for word — to be used in *Roots*. Too bad Haley didn't have a split screen.

I almost did the same thing with one of my earlier books. I copied material I thought was a taped interview but turned out to be material my secretary had copied from someone else's book. Horrors!

Now my computer instructor tells me I'll never have to face that problem again. With my split screen I can change just enough words that I never have to worry about going to jail.

But a question remains: Is it right?

It is the same question preachers face. For if plagiarism is an occasional problem for writers, it is a weekly problem for preachers.

For instance: Should pastors feel free to preach others' sermons? If they do, must they give credit for them?

And what about telling stories they've heard other people tell — and taking credit for the stories themselves?

To a certain degree, all of us preach other people's stuff. After all, as Solomon once said, there's not much new under the sun. Besides, so many in the pulpit today have to preach far beyond what they are creatively equipped to do. Using other pastors' sermons would be a great help. In fact, preaching sermons already preached by great pulpiteers would teach the rest of us a great deal about homiletics.

On the other hand, it makes me feel slightly uneasy to endorse something like this — which in many other realms would be considered plagiarism — without having a very good basis upon which I could do so.

Of course, in the strictest sense of the word, everyone plagiarizes. In fact, the preceding paragraph was plagiarized from the letter written me by Terry Muck, editor of LEADERSHIP, when he first suggested I write on this topic. I lifted it, word for word, and doubt if he or anyone else would have known the difference had I not called attention to it.

This brings up one of the primary reasons for not giving credit. Most speakers hate to break the flow in the middle of a message. It's much easier to keep going than to confuse the hearer with a score of footnotes plugged into the actual text.

But courtesy calls for gratefulness — as long as it can be given without distracting. Recently the leaders in our church have been studying Richard Foster's excellent book *Celebration of Discipline*. I heartily agree with much of what Foster has written and wish I had said it first. But for me to stand in the pulpit and take credit for what originated with him not only would be theft — it would be foolish. I would be quickly spotted carrying stolen goods. I would lose far more credibility (at least in the eyes of my leaders) than I would gain in the eyes of others who might be impressed with my brilliance.

Therefore, it is far easier to say, "I learned something this last week while studying Richard Foster's book *Celebration of Discipline*." Now I am free to take off on whatever tangent I wish. At the same time, I have pointed people back to the genesis of an idea. If they return to the spring to drink — as I have drunk — they, too, may come up with original thoughts, just as I did.

In my early days of preaching, I relied heavily on books of sermons and — perish the thought — books of sermon illustrations. Since a powerful experience with the Holy Spirit in 1968, I have not had to fall back on those. I discovered I had been preaching leftovers, while the Lord had set before me a banquet table from which I could feed the people. (This, by the way, is perhaps the strongest argument against preaching someone else's material. If it is not your own, if you have not experienced the truth you are preaching, how can it minister life to those who hear it?) But the spring inside me that flows with eternal truth sometimes gets clogged with debris. My pump, then, is often primed by the sermons of others, written, taped, or heard in person.

A preacher friend once joked: "When better sermons are written, I'll preach them."

To that I say, "Amen!"

In fact, I hope I am one who will write the better sermons — and that he will not only preach them but improve on them as he does. It is a humbling honor to know that something I originated is now in wider circulation because it is being told from various pulpits where I could never go.

There is a danger, however, in taking someone else's first-person experience and telling it as though it happened to you. This danger is especially acute in this day of mass media, when some of the people sitting in your congregation may have just heard the author tell the same story on national TV or may have just read the book you swiped your story from.

(Incidentally, those folks will not call you a *plagiarizer* when they get in the car and drive home after church. They'll call you a *liar*.)

Sometimes, of course, it works in the other direction. I remember when Charles Allen came to preach in the little South Carolina town where I was pastor of the Baptist church. I had read all of Allen's books of sermons — and preached most of them.

Some of our folks went down to Main Street Methodist to hear Dr. Allen. One of them came back and told me, "You'll never believe it, but that lanky old Methodist is preaching your sermons. He even told one of your stories last night and didn't have the decency to give you credit."

I held my breath until the week was over and Dr. Allen was safely out of town. At that time I was having enough trouble hiding other things without it being discovered I was stealing sermons as well.

The question is not whether we use material that originates with others. Of course we do. The question is whether we should give credit or not.

Sometimes we don't want to give credit. The author may be someone who has a bad reputation — or whose works might lead people astray. In such a case, I find it easy to say, "Although I certainly don't recommend the ideas of Hugh Hefner, I was intrigued by an interview in last night's paper where he said . . ."

On the other hand, giving credit often strengthens the message. It lets your people know you are reading — and listening. In short, it adds authenticity. Even though Richard Foster is a legitimate scholar in his own right, he is relatively unknown. Therefore, when he quotes Saint John of the Cross, Brother Lawrence, Dietrich Bonhoeffer, or his fellow Quaker Elton Trueblood, it adds credibility to his scholarship. In fact, had he not quoted so widely, many of us would not have read his books.

I am impressed when I attend a mainstream Protestant church and hear the speaker quote a charismatic or Roman Catholic — and give credit. I am attracted when I hear a Pentecostal quote a traditional evangelical. It lets me know the person is hearing what God is saying to the rest of Christendom. In short, the credits often mean as much as the material quoted.

"I was listening to a Charles Swindoll tape last week, and he told of the time . . ."

"I wish all of you would read Henri Nouwen's book *The Wounded Healer*. In the chapter on 'Ministry to a Hopeless Man,' he describes a fascinating encounter between . . ."

"A few years ago LEADERSHIP magazine interviewed Dr. Richard Halverson, chaplain of the U.S. Senate. In the interview . . ."

Perhaps the original material grew out of something informal, such as a staff meeting or home Bible study. If the originator of the idea is local, that is even more reason to give credit and thus encourage the person.

"Last Monday night in our home church meeting, Brooks Watson pointed out something he had learned a number of years ago in engineering school. . . ."

"In our staff meeting Art Bourgeois touched my heart when he began praying for . . ."

Giving credit, instead of distracting from your sermon, often leads your listeners into the situation. They wait eagerly to hear what you have gleaned from others.

Courtesy demands a certain amount of credit, and ethics demands you not retell a story as if it happened to you — unless it really did. If you're afraid the audience will think you stole a story when you didn't, a simple technique will get you off the hook. All you have to say is: "In his book *Where Eagles Soar*, Jamie Buckingham confesses the difficulty he had demonstrating physical love to his aged father. It brought to mind a similar experience I had with my own dad. . . ." From that point on, the story is yours, even though it might sound identical to the one I wrote about.

All preachers have a way of picking up cute phrases, vivid word images, clever bits of dialogue, even snappy one-liners they heard or read from someone else. Certainly Billy Graham didn't coin the phrase "The Bible says," but at least for this generation, he made it popular.

Such snatches are below the threshold of requiring attribution. But there is a level that enters the forbidden zone of plagiarism. It happens when we take credit for something valuable which is not genuinely ours.

Recently I heard a preacher at a ministerial convention tell an uproariously funny story of being invited to speak at a strange church and discovering, upon arrival, that it was a drive-in church. His congregation was a large field full of automobiles. He had no eye contact and no way of knowing if anyone was laughing at his jokes. His final dismay came when the pastor whispered in his ear that it was all right to give an invitation for people to accept Christ. He could even pray for the sick. If the people blinked their headlights, they had been saved. If they tooted the horn, they had been healed.

("Yes, dear brother, I see those headlights out there.")

I don't remember the point he was making, but his story was great. As we were leaving the auditorium, I overheard one pastor say to another, "I just got my illustration for next Sunday." I didn't ask, but I doubted seriously if he intended to give the original preacher credit for the story.

But for that matter, it doesn't make much difference. Back in 1974, Kenneth A. Markley, a Rosemead Graduate School psychologist, published the original story in his book *Our Speaker This Evening* (Zondervan). Dr. Markley, however, had not mentioned the horn blowing. That was added by the preacher to spice up an already good story and perhaps clear his conscience of being a plagiarist.

I wondered, walking away from the auditorium, how many preachers would add yet another twist — maybe turning on the windshield washers if you wanted counseling or releasing the hood latch if you wanted to donate to the visiting speaker's missionary fund.

Professional writers have strict guidelines concerning plagiarism. One definition is found in *A Handbook to Literature* by Thrall and Hibbard (Odyssey, 1960):

> Literary theft. A writer who steals the plot of some obscure, forgotten story and uses it as new in a story of his own is a

plagiarist. Plagiarism is more noticeable when it involves stealing of language than when substance only is borrowed. From flagrant exhibition of stealing both thought and language, plagiarism shades off into less serious things such as unconscious borrowing, borrowing of minor elements, and mere imitation.

Writers and musicians understand this. But while they can copyright words and notes, they cannot copyright an idea. It is in this area that the blacks and whites blend to gray, and each preacher must determine the difference between what is illegal, merely unethical, or permitted.

I remember asking a colleague if anyone ever plagiarized his sermons. He said, no, he'd never said anything worth repeating.

On the other hand, why would anyone publish a book of sermons if he didn't want them used?

Corrie ten Boom used to say that everything she had written or said was public property. She didn't want credit. She felt the glory should go to God, who gave her the ideas in the first place. She also felt copyrights were of the Devil. On occasion, her publishers had to hold her down, or she would have given carte blanche permission for anyone to reprint her material without even asking, much less paying a permission fee.

But Tante Corrie was a unique breed. She never did understand why someone would publish something "to the glory of God" and then get upset when another of God's servants used it without giving the author credit. After all, she used to say, that's why we put it in print in the first place — to be used.

On the other hand, she was always giving others credit. When she and I wrote *Tramp for the Lord*, I had to struggle to keep her from naming everyone she had ever talked to about an idea.

Perhaps that's a good rule to follow: Everything we say is free, and we expect nothing in return. For everything we borrow, we try to give credit — not because credit is due, but because God has a way of blessing honesty.

NINE

THE DAY
I BROUGHT
A SKUNK
TO CHURCH

The cure for dullness in the pulpit is not brilliance but reality.

P. T. FORSYTH

The common people are captivated more readily by comparisons and examples than by difficult and subtle disputations. They would rather see a well-drawn picture than a well-written book.

MARTIN LUTHER

In preaching, the best time to hook a congregation is at the outset. The moment is ripe. Catch it, and thoughts travel with you; lose it, and minds dim like lights in a brownout.

To begin a sermon with spark is half the battle. And a well-chosen illustration can ignite that spark.

Sometimes the illustrations practically write themselves. Those are the blessed Sundays. Other times, the dread monster, Sermon Block, rears its ugly head, scaring away any great beginnings — or even mediocre ones for that matter — and we wonder if we can get anything across before the congregation signals one by one that the lights are on but no one's home.

When he was pastor of Grace Chapel in Lexington, Massachusetts, Gordon MacDonald needed a desperate skunk to provide the perfect illustration for his sermon one Sunday.

In this chapter, MacDonald, now president of Inter-Varsity Christian Fellowship, does not simply tell how to illustrate; he illustrates it.

I was driving to church when I first saw the skunk in the middle of Grant Street, a quiet thoroughfare in my hometown of Lexington, Massachusetts. Skunks are a common sight in the early morning hours, but this one was different. It was violently careening back and forth from one curb to the other, blinded and crazed by what seemed to be a box jammed over its head.

I looked closer. The skunk had apparently raided someone's garbage can during the night, found a cocoa box with a few grains of chocolate in the bottom, and decided to pursue what refreshment remained. But greed had gotten the best of the animal when it stuck its nose far inside, and now the box had become a self-made prison.

This strange encounter with the skunk happened early on a beautiful Sunday morning, the sort of day that makes New Englanders glad they didn't relocate in Florida. If I felt a bit groggy that morning, it was because I'd struggled through one of those sleepless nights experienced by all preachers who aren't quite sure the Sunday morning sermon has jelled enough to be confidently delivered to a discriminating congregation.

Although I felt confident that I had something substantial and biblical to say, I was alarmed about the introduction. The fact was that it hardly existed. I had been unable to develop one that made sense. You could call it a preacher's version of "writer's block."

My fear was based on years of preaching experience, which have taught me that some sort of "key" is needed to open the doors of people's hearts. You can't simply stand up and say, "This is what I have on my mind today," and then expect everyone to be overwhelmed with curiosity. Perhaps a sergeant could get away with that in the army, but not a preacher in the pulpit.

That "key" can take many forms: a startling question, a humorous comment, the recollection of a common event, or a familiar story. Whatever key the speaker selects, it has to be provocative because it must break through all sorts of resistances set up in the minds of preoccupied, fatigued, and perhaps even bored people. That fact of preaching life was making me feel desperate that morning when I drove up Grant Street and met the skunk.

I stopped my car and spent several minutes in amusement at the skunk's predicament. I even entertained the notion of getting out of the car and relieving the skunk of its burden. But a smarter side of me concluded that the terrified animal might misunderstand my motive and act in the time-honored manner of all cornered skunks. As I watched from the safety of my car, he grew more exhausted and finally slowed his frantic pace, slinking off to one side of the road to ponder his untenable situation.

I drove past the skunk — on the other side of the road — and felt a faint sensation of guilt. Perhaps it was the kind of feeling that might have needled the priest and the Levite in the biblical story who, while traveling down the road to Jericho, chose to ignore a mugged man lying in a ditch. I also had my religious duties that morning, and I couldn't see how I could help the skunk anyway.

When our morning worship service began a couple of

hours later, the boxed-in skunk was all but forgotten. Here I was, just twenty minutes away from presenting an important challenge to the congregation, and I didn't know yet how to seize their attention.

What made matters worse for me was that it happened to be the first Sunday of our annual missions emphasis, and my objective in the sermon was to reaffirm our responsibility to share our faith and material resources with the poor and needy. And I needed no one to remind me that when it is a matter of people and money, you had better be able to do a superior job of persuasion.

I became more and more distressed as the worship service went on. It was uncharacteristic of me, I told myself, to be on the verge of entering the pulpit not knowing exactly how the sermon was to be launched. What had gone wrong in my preparation? Had I missed something God had wanted me to see or think through? Perhaps I'd failed to prepare the right sermon entirely.

It was sometime during the offering when the plight of the skunk reentered my mind. *What had happened to him?* I wondered. *And what would have happened to me if I'd tried out the Good Samaritan routine?*

Suddenly ideas began to converge. I could almost feel my imagination at work. Like it or not, that skunk was coming to our church. Well, in story form anyway.

A minute later I was at the pulpit. I began to describe what I'd seen on Grant Street a few hours before. I pictured the delight the skunk must have felt when he first found the cocoa box in a garbage can — and his frustration when he tried to reach the treat inside. But the hole was narrow, I reminded them, unaccommodating to a skunk's mouth. You could sense that as the story progressed the congregation was hooked. Even the children were hanging on every word. Everyone was trying to picture the skunk straining to get his tongue through the hole in the top of that cocoa box.

Then I described the unhappy result: how the skunk discovered to his horror that he and the box were suddenly inseparable. That's when I drove up — with the skunk out in the street, running amuck, desperate to free itself.

I waited for several seconds. It's the sort of self-imposed silence that makes a nervous speaker impatient. But the pause is important — listeners can let the words sink in like a soft rain until from somewhere down deep in the listeners' hearts, laughter begins. Uproarious laughter. My last-minute introduction had exceeded my fondest hopes. Everyone was involved — exactly what an effective introduction is supposed to do.

When the laughter ended, I went on, "You can now appreciate the fact that I was faced with a momentous moral dilemma."

You could almost see the wheels turning in a thousand minds, thinking through the implication of the comment. And then, an explosion of laughter; everyone got the point almost at the same time.

The "moral challenge" was obvious. They could smell a no-win situation without further explanation. And that is the stuff out of which humor is usually made.

I suppose they also laughed because something told each listener that there was enormous symbolism in the story. They were caused to think of even greater predicaments in which we all eventually find ourselves — similar moral challenges carrying even greater risks of disaster.

The congregation was thinking with me now. I had broken through their boredom, their preoccupations, their fatigue. A mental key had been turned with the story of the skunk, and all of them were fascinated to see how the preacher was going to use it.

With an opening tale as good as that one, the rest of any sermon, if properly prepared, can move swiftly for a preacher and even the congregation. In this case, the one thing that remained was to make sure the account of the skunk was properly linked with the overarching truth.

The purpose of the sermon had been to challenge the people to understand that caring for one another and for the people of the world who are oppressed and deprived is not only necessary, but probably involves sacrifice. And it may possibly be something that cannot be done without personal risk. "These were the sort of things that had been going in my mind when I asked myself if I shouldn't do something for that skunk on Grant Street."

But there was a final question to ask. By this time the congregation was sitting quietly, in fact intensely, thinking through the potential cost and casualties involved in caring. It became time to break that tension. So I said, "Now some of you are probably wondering what happened to the skunk."

I had caught them. The laughter said that was exactly what they had been wondering.

"The answer is simple," I said. "I don't know. Perhaps the police came and shot it." There were groans of dismay. "Perhaps someone braver came along and attempted a rescue. And perhaps," again I paused, "the skunk is up in the woods still facing a dangerous situation."

You could tell that the congregation had become quite sympathetic, and it grieved them to think that he was dead or that he remained in trouble.

Thus I posed this final question: "Why do you and I find it relatively easy to sympathize with a poor animal in a defenseless situation yet too often ignore human beings in a similar predicament?"

The question burned into each one of us. What were we to do about a world that included a lot of wounded and hurting people whose predicaments were similar to a frightened animal crazed and blinded by a self-contained prison? They were the ones we had to consider rescuing with our love, our energy, our resources. We could not afford to pass them by. With that, the sermon was over.

If I'd not been able to bring that skunk to church in story form, where would that sermon have ever gone? His plight had become my main point, and because of him, people began to think about caring in a new light.

The sun was noon-high as I drove back down Grant Street

after the worship services. When I reached the place where I'd met the skunk earlier in the morning, I slowed down just a bit to see if he might still be around. He wasn't.

I wonder what I would have done if he'd still been there. Would I have reciprocated the favor he paid me by coming to church in my sermon? Would I have been more caring about him the second time around? I never had a chance to find out.

Part IV
CONCLUDING

T E N

BUILDING BRIDGES TO ACTION

Good words without deeds
are rushes and reeds.

THOMAS FULLER

Life is Act,
and not to Do
is Death.

LEWIS MORRIS

Just as the fetching introduction pulls people into the sermon, the effective conclusion drives home the point and propels into the world people with an agenda.

A Rob Suggs cartoon in LEADERSHIP pictures a hapless pastor in front of a chart showing precipitously declining attendance. His companion suggests, "I'm no expert, Joe, but perhaps you shouldn't close each sermon with 'But then again, what do I know?' " The inappropriate ending can ruin even a great beginning.

But most preachers won't destroy a sermon with a foolish conclusion. The greater danger is losing an opportunity by not tapping a sermon's potential, by forfeiting the final push that makes a good sermon great and changes lives.

David Mains has a passion to change people's behavior. With dogged determination he returns to one overriding concern: Have I given people a way to act on their conviction? Some concrete way to put conviction to work? If not, he believes, he has not concluded properly. The sermon is incomplete.

Mains, many years a pastor at Chicago's Circle Church, now preaches on "The Chapel of the Air," a daily radio program originating in Carol Stream, Illinois. With brief minutes to communicate to an unseen audience, Mains now concentrates all the more on providing appropriate bridges from conviction to action. He shares his methods in this chapter.

I listen to a lot of other preachers — carefully, too. It's more than professional curiosity; I want to learn from both their strengths *and* their weaknesses.

I can usually determine the subject of the sermons I listen to. But often I'm confused about what I'm supposed to *do* or to *stop doing*. That's frustrating, especially since it's a rare text that doesn't call for an explicit response.

Sometimes I work with student preachers. Once they choose a text, I tell them to look for two things: the subject and the response being called for. I ask them to identify these two elements before they look for anything else in the passage. Why? Because the success of their preaching hinges on imparting not only the meaning but the imperative of a text.

When lay people tell me they heard a preacher and "Oh, he was good!" I often respond, "I'm pleased. Tell me, what was his subject?" Usually, with varying degrees of accuracy, they can answer.

"And what did he want you to do or to stop doing?" Now we're on a desert journey without water. Most people can't remember. Most likely, the preacher never stated the desired response.

The major component necessary for better preaching, I believe, is the imperative — the call for specific action arising from the sermon text.

Scribes or Preachers?

To what did the multitudes respond in Christ's preaching? After the Sermon on the Mount, Scripture records: "And when Jesus finished these sayings, the crowds were astonished at his teachings, for he taught them as one who had authority, and not as their scribes" (Matt. 7:28–29). There is a grand difference between a scribe and a preacher.

Comments you hear in sermons infected with what I call "the scribes' disease" include:

"Here's what so-and-so writes about these verses."

"A related passage that sheds light on this one is . . ."

"Those who want to dig deeper into God's truth would do well to probe this passage further."

Scribes tend to be fascinated with information. By contrast, preachers, like Christ, are more action oriented. For them, the word *sermon* means a *thrust*. "It's a thrust from the sword of the Spirit," writes Simon Blocker in *The Secret of Pulpit Power*. "And the preacher knows whether or not his thrust has been driven home."

I'm convinced many people say they like certain preachers not because they're helped to be different but because they found that speaker interesting, clever, able to project personality into his sermon. Their bottom line: *He wasn't boring and I enjoyed listening to him*. But were preachers meant to be entertainers?

People may leave a scribe's service pumped full of interesting new information. They can say how one verse relates to another or how the ethics of the Decalogue foreshadow the completion of the Beatitudes. But what a shame for them to leave church services unaware of what they are to do or to stop doing.

If someone wants to know how to play music, it does little

good for me to talk about the lives of famous composers, or to compare in detail the various instruments in the orchestra, or review how violins are made. It may make me sound learned and wise, but this person needs to be told, "Lesson one is on how to hold your flute. Between now and when we meet next week, I want you to practice holding it like this."

Most Christians I know don't need more information or "deeper truths." They haven't processed a fraction of the ones they already know. Profundity is not the crying need but simplicity coupled with directness: "Here's what my text is about and it's calling for us to do this."

I want my preaching to communicate specific responses to genuine needs felt by real people. And I find they respond favorably to such down-to-earth preaching anchored in their world. They don't particularly want more ideas. They aren't enamored with brilliant analysis or formal essays. I can't even assume they have a great love for theology or a vast reservoir of biblical knowledge.

I always ask the question: "What practical suggestions can I give to help people respond to what is said?" That's a watershed question. If I adequately address that question, my listeners will appreciate what they hear. And they'll be helped by it.

Bridges to Behavior

To make sure I am communicating, I have tried various methods, like brainstorming my sermons on Wednesday nights with a random group of parishioners invited to my home, or holding a pastor's class after Sunday worship to discuss the sermon. The people who have most shaped my sermons have not been ministers but parishioners gracious enough to not only listen but also critique what they heard.

In discussing my sermons with listeners, I've found it doesn't take long before they agree that the subject is relevant and the response called for in the passage is legitimate. But they say they need help with the "how to's." That's what the serious Christian comes to a sermon to hear.

"Don't talk anymore about the subject," they tell me. "I already agree with the biblical challenge to respond. Tell me how to pull it off! Can't you use your time building a bridge for me to get into this coveted new land?"

We preachers must build practical bridges. We need to list the first steps necessary to respond to what Scripture requires, and then we have to walk people over those bridges, step by step, to get them to that point.

For example, when Billy Graham preaches about conversion — being born again — he challenges his hearers to follow Christ. That's his desired response. Now how are they to do this? What's his bridge?

"What I want you to do," he tells them, "is to get up from where you are sitting and to walk down here to the front." He knows trained counselors are ready to talk with these people and lead them to Christ. It's a good bridge — "Here's how to do what I've been telling you about."

A number of other bridges lend themselves to evangelistic sermons. The traditional invitation is only one of many possibilities.

Some people find an immediate public response intimidating. They intend to respond — the Word has done its work — but making such a sudden decision and walking in front of all those people seems out of the question. For them I might devise bridges less threatening in a congregational setting, such as:

• Printing my phone number in the bulletin with specific hours I will be at the phone with the sole purpose of taking calls from those wanting to investigate the implications of becoming a Christian. Then I can point out the number and hours in my sermon.

• Providing cards on which they can write their phone number so I can call them. They may place the cards in the offering plate or give them to me at the door.

• Arranging a meeting after the service, sometimes over lunch, for any who want to continue working toward a decision.

- Making available inexpensive books they can either borrow or buy after the service. When they sign it out or pay for it, I then have a record of their interest or possible decision to use for follow-up. People will rarely seek out a bookstore to find a recommended book, but at the book table in the rear, they eagerly snatch up books on consignment from local bookstores.
- Challenging people to talk with a Christian of their choice about any decision they have made. Most know a mature believer whom they trust. I can offer to arrange such a meeting if they don't know anybody. They may find talking to a lay person less intimidating than a pastor.
- Making available cassette tapes to those who have made decisions, again getting their names for follow-up. Cassettes can help new believers firm their decisions. Although neither books nor cassettes provide all a new believer needs, telling people to take this step is a safe bridge to the action I ultimately desire: growth through involvement with other Christians.

Each of these alternatives builds a bridge to action. People can walk away from a service knowing something concrete to do if they have made a decision. They have their first steps outlined for them.

The use of bridges, however, is not limited to evangelistic sermons. *Every* sermon can benefit from suggested steps to action. Since the type of bridge depends on the response intended by the text, there are countless possibilities. When trying to determine what bridge to use for a particular sermon, the questions to ask are: *What response does the text demand?* and *How can I best move the people toward that response?*

When preaching on prayer, for example, I wanted people to learn to pray thankfully. I might have left it at that: "When you pray, be thankful." But that would have left most of them at a loss: "Thankful for what? And how do I pray thankfully?"

So I provided a bridge. I asked them to take a few minutes later that day to write out ten things they were thankful for. The next day they were to write out ten more, not repeating any from the first day, and on the third day ten more, until the week was up and they had a list of seventy blessings. I asked them to bring the list the next week, when we would talk about it some more. By the next Sunday, they were ready to hear more because they had acted on the first sermon.

For a sermon on addiction to pornographic materials, I asked the congregation if during the next week they were willing to throw away questionable mail before opening it, to destroy that hidden stash of unseemly materials, to avoid particular bookracks and magazines and theater marquees. Since pornography can be an addiction, I asked them to consider one more step they felt they could take to break its hold. The bridge took them from knowing what is bad to determining what to do in response.

For a recent series of broadcast sermons, I provided a simple graph for people to chart their day-to-day battle with a bad habit. People could choose the behavior they wanted to plot, and one woman wrote me of her experience fighting immorality. Although she was a Christian, she and her boyfriend were going to bed together regularly. It bothered her conscience, but she seemed unable to break the habit.

It was that problem she chose to plot on her graph. After one date that ended, inevitably, in bed, the next day with tears she marked her failure on the graph. She went several days without a problem and her graph started looking good. But then on another date she fell again. The simple task of having to graph another failure got to her. That's not how she wanted her graph to appear!

She made up her mind that this couldn't continue, so she talked with her boyfriend. He didn't necessarily agree, but he was willing to respect her decision. Her letter said it had been a number of weeks and she had retained a perfect record since that time. She knew all along she shouldn't be immoral. What she needed was a bridge to cross the deep divide between her knowledge and her desired actions.

A sermon by John Huffman at the Congress on Biblical Exposition stands out for me because he told me what to do and also provided me a bridge. His bridge was simple: Get into an accountability group. He told how he had done it and what it meant to him and his preaching. He shared his weakness and his need for counsel. I came away from his sermon with an idea of what he wanted me to do and how to do it.

Bridges take many forms. I watched an Episcopal priest finish a fine Good Friday sermon about the Cross by displaying two crucifixes and suggesting that all of us get one ourselves to help us remember the richness of propitiation and redemption — those big theological words that mean so little apart from the Cross. Even though I probably won't buy a crucifix, simply by viewing one again, I am moved beyond theological language to worship our Lord, whose agony for us a crucifix strongly portrays.

Supply a short list of Scriptures to be memorized; print a card with the sermon theme for people to carry in their wallets; suggest they evaluate a certain television show for its secular or Christian message; put a question in the bulletin for people to discuss over Sunday dinner — the bridges are varied. The common denominator is their specific practicality. They can be done immediately as a way to begin to put the sermon's message to work.

I have found through years of lay–preacher dialogue that if I can't tell my listeners what to do, if I can't construct good bridges for people, they probably won't figure out applications for themselves. I don't worry about sounding "Mickey Mouse." The specifics, the how to's, the practicalities belong in great exposition every bit as much as in Sunday school handouts.

When approaching a text, I can preach best by, first, zeroing in on the text's subject; second, extracting from the Scripture the response being called for; and third, from my Christian understanding, constructing a bridge that will help people get from where they are to where this text teaches they should be. I want to help them respond to the challenge of the passage.

According to a 1985 poll, 42 percent of the adults in America attend religious services in a typical week. If we can get those four in ten adults to leave our preaching services saying, "I know what God wants me to do, and I have been given a reasonable way to begin the process. I'm going to do it!" — if we can pull this off Sunday after Sunday — then our preaching will fulfill its purpose: God's Word will equip his people to begin *doing* his will.

ELEVEN

HOW TO GIVE AN HONEST INVITATION

The Word did everything. I did nothing.
The gospel simply ran its course.

MARTIN LUTHER

At a small-town community Thanksgiving Eve service attended by only a handful of church pillars, an evangelistic invitation might be superfluous. Yet the same community's Easter sunrise service, attracting the curious, the civilly religious, and those catching an early service for appearances, is hardly the place for vague talk and a dismissal. People need a way to respond to the message before blankets and chairs are returned to car trunks and a perfect opportunity is wasted.

Preachers laboring to convince worshipers about the most important topic — salvation — have long used the invitation as a way to solidify decisions. But when is the altar call appropriate and when is it not? How can it be done with integrity? Are there better ways for seekers to walk the sawdust trail?

Leighton Ford, long associated with the Billy Graham Evangelistic Association, has witnessed and conducted thousands of altar calls. He, too, has cringed at the misuses. For Ford, the altar call is more than simply a means to end a preaching service; it is a pointed tool to be used with skill and care.

N

ot a few of us have been turned off by public invitations that offended our theology, our integrity, our sensitivities.

Some "altar calls" I wish I hadn't heard, and I doubt they altered anyone. I recall a healing evangelist during my younger days who cajoled and threatened his audience until the number of people God had "revealed" to him came forward that night. But I also recall another man with a gift of healing who laid his hands gently but with authority on those who came to kneel at the altar of an Anglican church.

I remember an evangelist in the Wheaton College chapel whose finger swept the audience like an avenging angel; his invitation was so broad we felt we should come forward if we hadn't written our grandmother in the last week! He squeezed and pleaded as if Jesus were some kind of spiritual beggar rather than the royal Lord. But I have seen Billy Graham stand silently, arms folded, eyes closed, almost a bystander, as a multiracial throng of Africans, Europeans, and Asians surged forward in South Africa to stand together at the Cross.

How do we give an honest invitation?

The Real Inviter

First, we must be honest before God. The only right we have to ask people to commit their lives for time and eternity is that God is calling them. The gospel message is both an announcement and a command: It tells what God has done and calls people to respond. "God was reconciling the world to himself in Christ, not counting men's sins against them. And he has committed to us the message of reconciliation. We are therefore Christ's ambassadors, as though God were making his appeal through us. We implore you on Christ's behalf: Be reconciled to God" (2 Cor. 5:19–20). *God is making his appeal through us.*

I am to present his message faithfully and give his call, trusting him with the response and giving him the glory. My part is to be faithful; his part is to produce fruit.

During a series of meetings conducted by R. A. Torrey years ago, there was no response the first several nights. Homer Hammontree, the songleader, came to Torrey in distress. "Ham," the evangelist replied, " 'it is required in stewards, that a man be found faithful.' Good night; I am going to bed."

Then came a service with tremendous outpouring of the Spirit and a huge response. Hammontree was exultant. Again Torrey said quietly, "Ham, 'it is required in stewards, that a man be found faithful.' Good night; I am going to bed."

I find it hard to be as cool as that, but I do admire Torrey's sense of honest faithfulness to God.

Why Am I Doing This?

But then I must also be *honest with myself.* Why do I give an invitation? Because it's expected in my church or tradition? Because I need the affirmation of seeing people respond visibly?

Or, on the other hand, do I not give an invitation because I fear embarrassment if people don't respond? Or criticism because it's not part of my group's tradition?

The only proper reason to give an invitation is that God calls people to decision. From Moses ("Who is on the Lord's side?") through Elijah ("How long will you waver between two opinions?") to Peter ("Repent and be baptized, every one of you") and Paul ("I preached that they should repent and turn to God and prove their repentance by their deeds") —the scriptural tradition is crisis preaching that calls for a decision. It has been noted that almost everyone Jesus called, he called publicly. Picture him directing James and John to leave their boats . . . Zacchaeus to climb down from the tree . . . the cripple to rise and walk.

None of us has completely pure motives. We are a mixed people. That is why I must continually pray, "Lord, let me not give this invitation because I need to see results. Let me not shun it because I am afraid or because someone might criticize. I must give it solely because you love these people, you want them to know you, and you have told me to tell them that."

Up-Front and Open

Then I must be *honest with the audience*. Many people would like to know God, but no one has ever asked them clearly.

Tony Campolo, a Philadelphia sociologist, was seated at a state prayer breakfast next to the governor and found that he was sympathetic but had never committed himself to follow Christ.

"Why not?" asked Campolo.

The governor honestly replied, "No one ever asked me."

"Well, I'm asking you."

To his surprise, the governor responded, "OK, I will."

The Scriptures use many metaphors to describe the step of faith: coming, following, kneeling, opening, receiving, turning. An invitation is a symbolic expression of that spiritual reality. It is nothing more, nothing less — and we need to explain that.

When I ask people to come forward at the end of an evangelistic meeting, I try to make it clear what I am asking them to do. At the beginning of the sermon I may say something like this: "Tonight at the end of my talk I am going to ask you to do something about it, to express your decision. I am going to ask you to get up and come and stand here at the front. This is an outward expression of an inward decision.

"Just as you make a promise to someone, mean to keep it, and shake hands on it . . . just as a young couple come to love each other, want to give themselves to each other, and then openly express that covenant in a wedding . . . so I am asking you to express your commitment. There is nothing magical in coming forward. Walking down here doesn't make you a Christian. You could come down here a thousand times with your feet, and it would make no difference at all if that's all it were. But as you come here with your feet, you are saying with your heart, 'God, I am coming to you and leaving behind those things that are wrong and sinful. I am trusting Christ as my Savior, and I am coming to follow him in his church from tonight on.' "

People need to know what responding to your invitation means and what it doesn't mean. They need to know that they must be open Christians, not private believers, and that this is a way of expressing that. It is also important that they know it is not the only way. While confession is required (Rom. 10:9), nowhere does Scripture demand that people raise a hand, come forward, or sign a card to confess Christ.

In my evangelistic invitations, I usually say so. "You don't have to come forward to be a Christian, but you do have to confess Christ and follow him openly." Some people are almost too shy even to come to church or be part of a crowd, let alone ever to come forward. Some overscrupulous souls live all their lives with a scar because they didn't come forward at some particular invitation. They need to know they can come to God in the quiet sanctuary of their own hearts and then express it in the faithfulness of their living. But they also need to know there is something about the open expression that clinches and seals that inner faith.

Others need to be told honestly that they must not put off God's call. "Not to decide is to decide" may be a common saying, but it is true. To hear the Shepherd's voice and shut ourselves to the sound is spiritually dangerous. An honest invitation will say with tenderness but seriousness, "Now is the day of salvation."

Some need to hear that Jesus is an alternative, not an additive to the good life. Through the Cross, he offers free grace but not a cheap grace that has no cross for us. Our Lord is not the Great Need Meeter in the Sky. Our invitation is not "You have tried everything else. Now put a little Jesus in your life." Mickey Cohen, the Los Angeles racketeer, wanted to know why, if there were Christian politicians and Christian singers, he couldn't be a "Christian gangster"! It was news to Mickey that Jesus didn't come to ratify his sins but to save him from them.

More than One Method

How then to give the invitation? It should be prepared as carefully as the rest of the message and the worship.

Should an invitation be given at every service? Each pastor and evangelist will need to settle that according to circumstances. I think an invitation should be given regularly in churches of a size and situation where numbers of visitors and non-Christians are likely. Almost every Sunday morning at Hollywood Presbyterian Church, Lloyd Ogilvie says, "I know that in a congregation of this size, there are those whom God is calling."

Other preachers may need to sense the leading of the Spirit and extend the invitation at the times and seasons when pastoral work and visitation seem to indicate people are ready. Some churches, particularly in England and Australia, schedule monthly guest services, perhaps the first or last Sunday morning of the month, when members bring friends to whom they have been witnessing. They know an evangelistic presentation and appeal will be made.

Every invitation should be surrounded with specific prayer

that the Holy Spirit will direct people to Christ. Both the preacher and praying people in the seats should cultivate a spirit of prayer throughout the entire service. Evangelism is a spiritual battle, and I am convinced that unbelief and indifference can create a field of resistance. Faith and prayer, on the other hand, can contribute to an atmosphere of expectancy and response.

An honest invitation, in my judgment, should begin at the outset of the message. People should know what is going to happen rather than having something sprung on them. Billy Graham begins giving the invitation with his opening prayer. I have already explained my approach. Then the invitation is repeated throughout the message as the truth is applied. I do not mean people are told over and over to take some action, but repeatedly they are asked, "Is this you? Has God been speaking to you about this and this? Are you sensing that God is calling you?"

Many good methods have been used. The simple, straightforward appeal to walk to the front and stand or kneel during the singing of a hymn is often effective. Following the example of some English evangelists, I sometimes use an "after-meeting," in which the congregation is dismissed and requested to leave while all interested people are invited to remain for a ten-minute explanation of how to make a Christian commitment. In some Lutheran churches, people are invited to come kneel at the altar or to take the pastor's hand as they leave and quietly say, "I will," if they are responding to the gospel appeal.

I have seen Vance Havner ask people to stand one at a time and openly say, "Jesus is my Lord," particularly in an invitation for rededication. At some evangelistic luncheons or dinners, blank three-by-five cards are on the tables, and everyone is asked to write a comment at the same time. Those who have invited Christ into their lives during a prayer are asked to include their names and addresses as an indication of their decision. It may be helpful to have those persons bring their cards to the speaker or leader, which could then open up personal conversation and counseling.

At First Presbyterian Church in Winston-Salem, North Carolina, worshipers who desire prayer for healing or problems are invited to come at the close of the service and kneel at the altar rail for prayer. It would be easy to add an invitation to those who wish to become Christians to join them.

There is no one way to extend the invitation, but in every situation there is surely some way. The essential elements are opportunities for (1) directed prayer and (2) simple biblical counseling. In a large evangelistic meeting, those who come forward may be led in a group prayer, but that is not enough. They need to express their faith to God individually before leaving.

In my crusades, counselors are instructed to come forward at the beginning of the invitation. Why? Not to prime the pump but to assist people, for it can be scary to walk forward publicly and particularly to stand alone. So there is no misunderstanding, I explain openly that these are counselors who are coming to lead the way. Lloyd Ogilvie often has selected elders stand at the front during the closing hymn to welcome those who respond. In any case, counselors should be trained ahead of time and provided with simple literature on the basics of the Christian faith and walk. Their interaction with people deciding to follow Christ can happen at the front of the church or in a quiet room nearby. Quick and dependable follow-up in the next forty-eight hours both by telephone and a visit in person must also take place.

Some Do's and Don'ts

In giving the invitation, *do* pick up the feelings of those in the throes of decision. Empathize with their fear of embarrassment, of not being able to follow through, of what others will say. Hear the inner voice that tells them this is too hard, or they can wait — it's not important. *Don't* berate or threaten. *Do* explain very simply what it is you are asking people to do. If you want them to get up, walk forward, stand at the front, face you, and wait until you have had a prayer, tell them exactly what will happen.

Don't use "bait and switch" — asking them only to raise their hand, and then only to stand, and then only to come forward. This is not to say we should never give an invitation in two steps, but it does mean we must not trick people or make them feel used.

Do make the meaning of the invitation clear. I don't think it's wrong to give an invitation with several prongs: salvation, rededication, renewal. I do think it's wrong to make it so vague that it's meaningless. *Don't*, on the other hand, over-explain so you confuse.

Do wait patiently, giving people time to think and pray, knowing the inner conflicts they may be facing. Sometimes those moments seem agonizingly slow for you, but be patient. *Don't*, however, extend and prolong when there is no response, saying "Just one more verse" twenty times, until the congregation groans inwardly for someone to go forward so you'll stop. *Do* encourage and urge people gently, repeating your invitation once or perhaps twice. But *don't* preach your sermon again.

Do give the invitation with conviction, with courage, with urgency, with expectancy. But *don't* try to take the place of the Holy Spirit.

To find balance in these matters is not easy. I find it helps if I ask God to speak to me as well as through me.

What if no one responds? Do you feel embarrassed? Have you fallen flat on your face? You may. I have felt that any number of times. But the embarrassment passes, and what remains is the conviction that you have given an honest invitation to the glory of God, and even if no one responded, they faced the decisiveness of confronting Christ. Who knows when what they have seen and heard will be used to bring them to faith?

And if people do respond? You can rejoice and pray that they will follow Jesus in the fellowship of his church and the tasks of their daily lives.

T W E L V E

FIVE TEMPTATIONS
OF THE PULPIT

*The paradox of the pulpit is that its
occupant is a sinner whose chief right to
be there is his perpetual sense that he has
no right to be there, and is there by grace
and always under a spotlight of divine
judgment.*

A. C. CRAIG

After the sermon is finished, the church doors locked, and the roast eagerly devoured, we start to unwind from another Sunday morning. During the sermon, all thought was on getting it said. Immediately following, there were hands to shake and people to see. Finally, though, some time during the next several hours, the questions begin rising to the surface:

How did I do?

Did I convince anyone?

Was the Word heard?

We begin to reflect on whether or not the sermon worked. A sermon that fails is emotionally devastating. The sermon that works, however, can be just as spiritually devastating. Holding sway is a heady thing. Producing conviction may well convince a preacher of his own greatness — a terrible price to pay for success.

At Irvine (California) Presbyterian Church, Ben Patterson fights a weekly battle with the twin devastations as well as the other ever-present pulpit temptations. His transparency in this chapter allows us a glimpse at the temptations we, too, face — temptations to rail at the saints, to use rather than absorb Scripture, to "grandstand" for the crowd.

Patterson demonstrates that quality of effective preachers: the ability to sort through a sermon in retrospect, finding satisfaction in the good and continuing to work on the rest.

I t was years ago, early in my preaching ministry. I made a broad gesture to the right, and every eye swung that direction. *Wow!* I thought to myself. *I can do that to people!* That marked the beginning of my acquaintance with the unique temptations of preaching.

Performing While You Preach

The first and greatest temptation is the one I experienced that day — to be a performer in the pulpit. In one sense, that's exactly what you must do when you preach — perform. Anyone who dares get up in front of a group of people and take twenty-five minutes of their time to deliver a monologue must be something of a ham. If you loathe that kind of exercise, chances are you will not be effective as a preacher.

But there's the catch. To preach well, you must constantly open yourself up to the deadliest temptation of the preacher: to put on a performance that will draw the applause and appreciation of the audience. There is no problem in all this if the audience, for you, is God. But unfortunately, God is not usually easy to see. What we do see is the crowd of people sitting in the pews. They are very easy to see, and too often the ones whose approval we seek.

Jesus laid his finger on this temptation in the sixth Beatitude: "Blessed are the pure in heart, for they shall see God." A pure heart is one with unmixed motives. Søren Kierkegaard says a pure heart wills one thing — to do the will of God, seeking his approval. That's why Jesus looked at the Pharisees, who did their good works to be thought well of by others, and said, "They have their reward." They were getting just what they were looking for: human approval.

Look for God, and you will see him. Look for people, and you will see them.

John Bunyan once preached an especially powerful sermon. The first person he spoke to afterward told him so. He said, "Yes, I know. The Devil told me that as I walked away from the pulpit." I cannot count the number of times I have stood outside the door of the sanctuary after I have preached, ravenous for the praise of my congregation. I had worked hard the previous week to be well prepared. I gave the delivery every bit of energy and concentration I could muster. In many ways I brought to the pulpit all the intensity I would bring to racquetball. Now I am even drenched in perspiration underneath my robe. I want to know, did I win?

In moments of clarity, I know only God can make that judgment and hand out the trophy. But it seems that things are rarely very clear to me after I have preached. Bruce Thielemann put it accurately when he wrote, "Preaching is the most public of ministries and, therefore, the most conspicuous in its failure and the most subject to the temptation of hypocrisy."

Preaching the Words of God

A second temptation for the preacher is to hear the Word of God only as something to be preached. The pressure to produce a sermon, combined with the fact that sermons are to be preached out of the Bible, can render impossible a simple reading of the Bible for its own sake, or for your own sake.

Every time I pick up the Bible and begin to get some insight into a particular passage, I immediately start thinking of how I can preach it to my congregation. I almost always by-pass its relevance to myself. That is deadly. Paul the apostle alluded to his struggle with this temptation when he expressed his concern that "after preaching to others I myself will not be disqualified" (1 Cor. 9:27).

The Book of James uses the metaphor of a mirror to describe the Word of God. The purpose of a mirror is to reveal an image: yours. In his brilliant essay "For Self-Examination," Kierkegaard described how people will examine the mirror, measure the mirror, list its properties, write dissertations on the uses of a mirror; in short, do everything and anything but look at the person the mirror would reveal! So it is with preachers who hear God's Word only as something to preach to someone else.

Preaching that has integrity comes from men and women who have wrestled personally with what they are proclaiming publicly. I fall prey to this temptation so easily that I must discipline myself to study passages devotionally before I attempt to sermonize on them. And I must do this months in advance of the actual preaching.

Turning Stones into Bread

A third temptation for the preacher is to try to turn stones into bread, to give people what they want instead of what they need. Because the preacher is, in one sense, a performer, there is always present in his psyche the desire to be liked and appreciated by those he preaches to. That desire can become so strong that he becomes as sensitive as a seismograph to the audience's tastes. It is at this point that the preacher can turn into a propagandist.

All propagandists really do is convince you that the thing you want will be furthered by their products, their candidates, or their messages. Whenever the gospel is portrayed as something that will help people get what they want, uncritical of what they want, it is made an instrument of propaganda. "The Bible has to define your needs before it meets them," said James Daane. "It has to tell you what you need — the nature of your hurts, pains, aches. In other words, the Bible has got to tell you what sin is, because you don't know."

A variety of this temptation to give people what they want is the overuse of stories and illustrations. Everyone who preaches knows how effectively a good story or joke gets people's attention. The problem with stories is that they lend themselves so readily to being interpreted any way the hearer wants. A congregation of widely divergent points of view can hear a sermon filled with a lot of entertaining stories, and everyone will leave the sanctuary feeling edified. The pastor really told it "like it is." Of course, if everybody's point was made, no point was made. But the pastor came off sounding good to everyone.

Prophet and Priest

A fourth temptation for the preacher is the opposite of the one just outlined. It is the temptation to fancy oneself something of a prophet to the people, and to do so at the expense of also being their priest. A prophet, as we all learned in school, is one who stands before the people on behalf of God. A priest is one who stands before God on behalf of the people. Prophets are mouthpieces. Priests are intercessors. Prophets confront the people with God's truth and their lies. Priests hold up the people before God's grace.

The temptation of being a prophet at the expense of being a priest is that you can blast away at your people from a position of splendid isolation. You don't have to go through the agony of caring for the ones you wound with the truth. You can sit in your study, do your exegesis, and give them the whole truth and nothing but the truth. But the truth you give might bludgeon someone without leading on to healing.

John tells us that Jesus came with grace and truth. Among other things, that means the Word became flesh and walked among us. It was no disembodied truth, but it came incarnate in one who shared our flesh and walked in our shoes. As the writer to the Hebrews put it, Jesus was a high priest who was not "unable to sympathize with our weaknesses, but one who in every respect has been tempted as we are . . ." (4:15).

A preacher simply does not have the right to blast away at his people with the truth — especially if it is the kind of truth that wounds — unless that preacher is also himself wounded by that truth and heartbroken over the plight of his people. A very wise old pastor once told me of two equal and opposite errors a preacher can fall into. One was to neglect his study for his people. The other was to neglect his people for his study. Both errors are tragic. People and study are in constant tension and competition with each other. But both must be attended to.

Making the Bible Relevant

I offer one last temptation of the preacher. It is the temptation to try to make the Bible relevant, to make it come alive. This particular temptation used to be the sole province of the liberal theological tradition. But in the past few years, it has gained a number of victims in the evangelical community.

I succumb to this temptation whenever I feel the Bible needs my help to be believed, that somehow it requires my zinger illustration or my perceptive restatement into thought forms more familiar to my congregation. Most often today those thought forms are the categories and vocabulary of pop psychology.

The sin courted in this temptation is the presumption that it is the Bible that is dead and we who are alive. Of course no preacher would admit to that formal proposition. But many act as though they believe it.

Is the Bible relevant? Dr. Bernard Ramm once remarked, "There is nothing more relevant than the truth." The longer I preach, the more convinced I become that the best thing I can do is simply get out of Scripture's way. The soundest homiletical advice I know is not to try to preach it well but just to try not to preach it badly.

This does not mean the preacher should not translate the message of the Bible in words people can understand. But the purpose should always be to help them see the relevance of the Scriptures, not make the Scriptures relevant. In the final analysis, the Word of God authenticates itself through the work of the Holy Spirit, often in spite of, not because of, us preachers.

One might conclude from this chapter that to be a preacher is to walk into a minefield of temptations. It is. I don't think I have ever preached a sermon with even 30 percent good intentions. And I have despaired as I have looked inside myself and seen the many ways I have fallen before the temptations of the preacher. If the purity of my motivations were the basis of my being in the pulpit, I would have been kicked out long ago. But, thank God, that is not the basis. The basis is the call of God. I am there only because he summoned me many years ago, gave me the necessary gifts, and said, "Start talking about me."

In our liturgy we confess our sins corporately, before we hear the Word of God through the reading and preaching of the Bible. I must also do so afterward. That is the pattern for me: confess, preach, confess again; and pray Martin Luther's sacristy prayer:

Lord God, you have made me a pastor in your church. You see how unfit I am to undertake this great and difficult office, and if it were not for your help, I would have ruined it all long ago. Therefore I cry to you for aid. I offer my mouth and my heart to your service. I desire to teach the people — and for myself, I would learn ever more and diligently meditate on your Word. Use me as your instrument, but never forsake me, for if I am left alone I shall easily bring it all to destruction. Amen.

THIRTEEN

YOUR PREACHING IS UNIQUE

The character of our praying will determine the character of our preaching. Light praying makes light preaching.

E. M. BOUNDS

A preacher reading about how to preach better can easily begin to feel like the farmer who finally refused to go to any more farm extension courses. His reason: "I don't need to learn any more. I already know how to farm better than I do now!"

Reading about the great ideas and wonderful successes of other preachers can be intimidating — the pastor who prepares sermons months early, the one packing in a thousand people compared to my fifty-five, the preacher with the seemingly inexhaustible supply of fresh stories, the witty one, the creative one, or the scholarly one. There will always be someone who preaches better. Always.

So why try? What good is my preaching compared to theirs?

Warren Wiersbe rides to the rescue of all who are ready to shelve their Bibles. Besides three decades of parish ministry, Wiersbe draws from an extensive conference, broadcast, and writing ministry. He's experienced the preacher's doldrums. He's been intimidated by the gifts of others.

But he can also put those feelings in perspective and celebrate the uniqueness of the individual preacher. And he tells each of us, whom God has tapped to proclaim his Word, "Indeed, your preaching is unique."

I t really doesn't make sense!"

That statement was made to me by a pastor friend about a dozen years ago. We were lingering over our lunchtime coffee and discussing the Bible conference I was conducting in his church. I'd just commented that the church was having a strong influence on the students and staff of the nearby university.

"What doesn't make sense?" I asked.

"Where you and I are serving," he replied.

"You are going to have to explain."

"Look, I'm really a country preacher with a minimum of academic training, yet I'm ministering to a university crowd. You write books, and you read more books in a month than I do in a year; yet your congregation is primarily blue-collar and nonprofessional. It doesn't make sense."

The subject then changed, but I have pondered his observation many times in the intervening years. I've concluded it's a good thing God didn't put me on his "Pastor Placement Committee" because I would have really messed things up. I'd never have sent rustic Amos to the affluent court of the king; I'd have given him a quiet country church somewhere. And

I'd never have commissioned Saul of Tarsus, that "Hebrew of the Hebrews," to be a missionary to the Gentiles; I'd have put him in charge of Jewish evangelism in Jerusalem.

All of which brings me to the point of this chapter: If God has called you to preach, then who you are, what you are, and where you are also must be a part of God's plan. You do not preach in spite of this but because of this.

Preaching and the Preacher

Why is it, then, that so many preachers do not enjoy preaching? Why do some busy themselves in minor matters when they should be studying and meditating? Why do others creep out of the pulpit after delivering their sermon, overwhelmed with a sense of failure and guilt? Without pausing to take a poll, I think I can suggest an answer: They are preaching *in spite of* themselves instead of preaching *because of* themselves. They either leave themselves out of their preaching or fight themselves during their preparation and delivery; this leaves them without energy or enthusiasm for the task. Instead of thanking God for what they do have, they complain about what they don't have; and this leaves them in no condition to herald the Word of God.

A CHRISTIANITY TODAY/Gallup Poll showed that ministers believe preaching is the number one priority of their ministries, but it's also the one thing they feel least capable of doing well. What causes this insecure attitude toward preaching?

For one thing, we've forgotten what preaching really is. Phillips Brooks said it best: Preaching is the communicating of divine truth through human personality. The divine truth never changes; the human personality constantly changes — and this is what makes the message new and unique. No two preachers can preach the same message because no two preachers are the same. In fact, no *one* preacher can preach the same message twice if he is living and growing at all. The human personality is a vital part of the preaching ministry.

Recently I made an intensive study of all the Greek verbs

used in the New Testament to describe the communicating of the Word of God. The three most important words are: *euangelizomai*, "to tell the good news"; *kērussō*, "to proclaim like a herald"; and *martureō*, "to bear witness." All three are important in our pulpit ministry. We're telling the good news with the authority of a royal herald, but the message is a part of our lives. Unlike the herald, who only shouted what was given to him, we're sharing what is personal and real to us. The messenger is a part of the message because the messenger is a witness.

God prepares the man who prepares the message. Martin Luther said that prayer, meditation, and temptation make a preacher. Prayer and meditation will give you a sermon, but only temptation — the daily experiences of life — can transform that sermon into a message. It's the difference between the recipe and the meal.

I had an experience at a denominational conference that brought this truth home to me. During the session at which I was to speak, a very capable ladies trio sang. It was an up-tempo number, the message of which did not quite fit my theme; but, of course, they had no way of knowing exactly what I would preach about. I was glad my message did not immediately follow their number because I didn't feel the congregation was prepared. Just before I spoke, however, a pastor in a wheelchair rolled to the center of the platform and gave a brief testimony about his ministry. Then he sang, to very simple accompaniment, "No One Ever Cared for Me Like Jesus." The effect was overwhelming. The man was not singing a song; he was ministering a Word from God. But he had paid a price to minister. In suffering, he became a part of the message.

The experiences we preachers go through are not accidents; they are appointments. They do not interrupt our studies; they are an essential part of our studies. Our personalities, our physical equipment, and even our handicaps are all part of the kind of ministry God wants us to have. He wants us to be witnesses as well as heralds. The apostles knew this: "For we cannot but speak the things which we have seen and heard" (Acts 4:20). This was a part of Paul's commission: "For thou shalt be his witness unto all men of what thou hast seen and heard" (Acts 22:15). Instead of minimizing or condemning what we are, we must use what we are to bear witness to Christ. It is this that makes the message *our* message and not the echo of another's.

It's easy to imitate these days. Not only do we have books of sermons, but we have radio and television ministries and cassettes by the thousands. One man models himself after Spurgeon, another after A. W. Tozer; and both congregations suffer.

Alexander Whyte of Edinburgh had an assistant who took the second service for the aging pastor. Whyte was a surgical preacher who ruthlessly dealt with man's sin and then faithfully proclaimed God's saving grace. But his assistant was a man of different temperament, who tried to move the gospel message out of the operating room into the banquet hall. However, during one period of his ministry he tried Whyte's approach but not with Whyte's success. The experiment stopped when Whyte said to him, "Preach your own message." That counsel is needed today.

Mixing Parish and Personality

I am alarmed when I hear seminary students and younger pastors say, "My calling is to preach, not to pastor." I am alarmed because I know it's difficult to preach to people whom you do not know. As an itinerant Bible teacher, I know what it's like to "hit a place and quit a place," and I can assure you it is not easy. After thirty years of ministry, which included pastoring three churches, I've concluded it is much easier to preach to your own congregation week after week. You get to know them, and they get to know you. You're not a visiting evangelical celebrity but a part of the family. It is this identification with the people that gives power and relevance to your preaching.

Every profession has its occupational hazards, and in the

ministry it is the passion to preach "great sermons." Fant and Pinson, in *Twenty Centuries of Great Preaching*, came to the startling conclusion that "Great preaching is relevant preaching." By "relevant," they mean preaching that meets the needs of the people in their times, preaching that shows the preacher cares and wants to help. If this be true, then there are thousands of "great sermons" preached each Lord's Day, preached by men whose names will never be printed in homiletics books but are written in the loving hearts of their people. Listen again to Phillips Brooks:

> The notion of a great sermon, either constantly or occasionally haunting the preacher, is fatal. It hampers . . . the freedom of utterance. Many a true and helpful word which your people need, and which you ought to say to them, will seem unworthy of the dignity of your great discourse. . . . Never tolerate any idea of the dignity of a sermon which will keep you from saying anything in it which you ought to say, or which your people ought to hear.

Let me add another reason for insecure feelings about our preaching. In our desire to be humble servants of God, we have a tendency to suppress our personalities lest we should preach ourselves and not Christ. While it is good to heed Paul's warning ("For we preach not ourselves, but Christ Jesus the Lord; and ourselves your servants for Jesus' sake" 2 Cor. 4:5), we must not misinterpret it and thereby attempt the impossible. Paul's personality, and even some of his personal experiences, are written into the warp and woof of his epistles; yet Jesus Christ is glorified from start to finish.

During the past twenty years, I have been immersed in studying the lives and ministries of the famous preachers of the past. Most of these men ministered during the Victorian Era in Great Britain, a time when the pulpits were filled with superstars. If there's one thing I learned from these men it is this: God has his own ways of training and preparing his servants, but he wants all of them to be themselves. God has put variety into the universe, and he has put variety into the church.

If your personality doesn't shine through your preaching, you're only a robot. You could be replaced by a cassette player and perhaps nobody would know the difference. Do not confuse the art and the science of preaching. Homiletics is the science of preaching, and it has basic laws and principles that every preacher ought to study and practice. Once you've learned how to obey these principles, then you can adapt them, modify them, and tailor them to your own personality.

In my conference ministry, I often share the platform with gifted men whose preaching leaves me saying to myself, *What's the use? I'll never learn how to preach like that!* Then the Lord has to remind me he never called me "to preach like that." He called me to preach the way I preach. The science of preaching is one thing; the art of preaching — style, delivery, approach, and all those other almost indefinable ingredients that make up one's personality — is something else. One preacher uses humor and hits the target; another attempts it and shoots himself.

The essence of what I am saying is this: You must know yourself, accept yourself, and develop yourself — your best self — if preaching is to be an exciting experience in your ministry. Never imitate another preacher, but learn from him everything you can. Never complain about yourself or your circumstances, but find out why God made things that way and use what he has given you in a positive way. What you think are obstacles may turn out to be opportunities. Stay long enough in one church to discover who you are, what kind of ministry God has given you, and how he plans to train you for ministries yet to come. After all, he is always preparing us for what he already has prepared for us — if we let him.

Realistic Evaluation

I learned very early in my ministry that I was not an evangelist. Although I've seen people come to Christ through my ministry, I've always felt I was a failure when it came to evangelism. One of the few benefits of growing older is a better perspective on life. Now I'm learning that my teaching and writing ministries have enabled others to lead people to Christ, so my labors have not been in vain. But I've had my hours of discouragement and the feeling of failure that always accompanies discouragement.

God gives us the spiritual gifts he wants us to have; he puts us in the places where he wants us to serve; and he gives us the blessings he wants us to enjoy. I am convinced of this, but this conviction is not an excuse for laziness or for barrenness of ministry. Knowing I am God's man in God's place of ministry has encouraged me to study harder and do my best work. When the harvests were lean, the assurance that God put me there helped to keep me going. When the battles raged and the storm blew, my secure refuge was "God put me here and I will stay here until he tells me to go." How often I've remembered Dr. V. Raymond Edman's counsel: "It is always too soon to quit!"

It has been my experience that the young preacher in his first church and the middle-aged preacher (in perhaps his third or fourth church) are the most susceptible to discouragement. This is not difficult to understand. The young seminarian marches bravely into his first church with high ideals, only to face the steamroller of reality and the furnace of criticism. He waves his banners bravely for a year or so, then takes them down quietly and makes plans to move. The middle-aged minister has seen his ideals attacked many times, but now he realizes that time is short and he might not attain to the top thirty of David's mighty men.

God help the preacher who abandons his ideals! But, at the same time, God pity the preacher who is so idealistic he fails to be realistic. A realist is an idealist who has gone through the fire and been purified. A skeptic is an idealist who has gone through the fire and been burned. There is a difference.

Self-evaluation is a difficult and dangerous thing. Sometimes we're so close to our ministry we fail to see it. One of my students once asked me, "Why can't I see any spiritual growth in my life? Everybody tells me they can see it!" I reminded him that at Pentecost no man could see the flame over his own head, but he could see what was burning over his brother's head. A word from the Scottish preacher George Morrison has buoyed me up in many a storm: "Men who do their best always do more though they be haunted by the sense of failure. Be good and true; be patient; be undaunted. Leave your usefulness for God to estimate. He will see to it that you do not live in vain."

Be realistic as you assess your work. Avoid comparisons like the plague. I read enough religious publications and hear enough conversation to know that such comparisons are the chief indoor sport of preachers, but I try not to take them too seriously. "When they measure themselves by themselves and compare themselves with themselves, they are not wise" (2 Cor. 10:12). Whoever introduced the idea of competition into the ministry certainly assisted the enemy in his attack against the church. Although we are in conflict against those who preach a false gospel, we are not in competition with any who preach the true gospel. We are only in competition with ourselves. By the grace of God, we ought to be better preachers and pastors today than we were a year ago.

If we are to be better pastors and preachers, we must be better persons; and this means discipline and hard work. The "giants" I've lived with these many years were all hard workers. Campbell Morgan was in his study at six o'clock in the morning. His successor, John Henry Jowett, was also up early and into the books. "Enter your study at an appointed hour," Jowett said in his lectures to the Yale divinity students in 1911–1912, "and let the hour be as early as the earliest of your businessmen goes to his warehouse or his office." Spurgeon worked hard and had to take winter holidays to regain his strength. Obviously, we gain nothing by imperiling our health, but we lose much by pampering ourselves, and that is the greater danger.

If God has called you, then he has given you what you need to do the job. You may not have all that others have, or all you wish you had, but you have what God wants you to have.

Accept it, be faithful to use it, and in due time God will give you more. Give yourself time to discover and develop your gifts. Accept nothing as a handicap. Turn it over to God and let him make a useful tool out of it. After all, that's what he did with Paul's thorn in the flesh.

Often I receive letters and telephone calls from anxious chairmen of pulpit committees, all of whom want me to suggest a pastor for their churches. "What kind of a pastor do you need right now?" I always ask, and the reply usually comes back, "Oh, a man who is about forty years old, a good preacher, evangelical. . . ." If I don't interrupt them, they usually go on to describe a combination of Billy Graham, Charles Spurgeon, Jonathan Edwards, Mother Teresa, and The Lone Ranger.

"Forgive me," I usually say when they take a breath, "but that's not what I had in mind. What kind of ministry does your church need just now — evangelism, missions, administration, teaching, or what? After all, very few pastors can do everything."

The long silence that follows tells me that Brother Chairman and his committee have not really studied their church to determine its present and future needs. How, then, can they ever hope to find the right pastor to meet those needs?

Preaching is not what we do; it's what we are. When God wants to make a preacher, he has to make the person, because the work we do cannot be isolated from the life we live. God prepares the person for the work and the work for the person and, if we permit him, he brings them together in his providence. Knowing we are God's person, in God's place of choosing, to accomplish God's special work ought to be sufficient encouragement for us to weather the storm and do our very best. God knows us better than we know ourselves. He'd never put us into a ministry where he could not build us and use us.